My Revenge

By Eugene Davis

My Revenge

Copyright © by Eugene Davis

Published in the United States by Davidovich Press

ISBN-13: 978-1533538543
ISBN-10: 1533538549

Davidovich Press
2402 Equadorian Way
Clearwater, Florida 33763

Dedication

This memoir is dedicated to my parents, Jacob (Yaakov) Mendel Davidovitch, a'h, and Rachel ne' Zola Davidovitch, a'h and sister Sari a'h , Hedi a'h, and Joseph a'h her two adorable children.

I mourn their deaths every day.

Their lives were cut short just because they were Jews. I will never know what could have been possible if they had been allowed to live out their days.

It's bad enough that the Nazis murdered my parents. I don't even have a grave I can visit to pay them my respect, as I visit my beloved wife's gravesite every week.

It's like they never existed.

But they did live, and they are in my thoughts every day. I hope they are resting in peace, and proud of the family I was privileged to raise with my life partner, Rose, a'h.

Acknowledgements

Many thanks to Azriela Jaffe. Without her patience, skillful interviews, and writing expertise this book would not be possible.

Table of Contents

Preface

I didn't speak much about the war unless asked. It wasn't just me. A whole generation of Jews after the Holocaust never talked about it. Until Eli Wiesel came out with his book, "Night". That book got a lot of survivors talking. Some survivors didn't want to talk about the war because they felt guilty about surviving. So many lost their entire families and communities and they couldn't stop asking the question, "why did I survive while so many good Jews did not?".

I didn't ask that question so much. From my family, we lost our parents and my sister with two adorable children (she wouldn't leave the children, even though neighbors offered to hide them).

I was one of the lucky ones. Before the war, my oldest sister and older brother were already living in the USA, and four of my siblings (three sisters and a brother) survived the concentration camps. I was spared the entire concentration camp ordeal, and I did not emerge from the war alone. Most of my siblings were alive, even if I was made an orphan.

I suffered plenty, as you will soon read. But from the time the war was over, and especially once I was in America, my focus was on how to rebuild my life. I always felt that by doing so, this was my greatest revenge against the Nazis, and my best way to fool Hitler.

Although I didn't spend a lot of time talking about the Holocaust when I was raising my son and daughter, I did make sure that they were all very well informed about Jewish causes, world Jewry, and Israel. My son and grandson are very active in AIPAC (American Israel Public Affairs Committee), even lobbying in Washington on their behalf. My daughter went to University in Israel.

Going through the Holocaust made me an ardent Zionist (I was really a Zionist before the war!). If Israel existed before the Holocaust, 6 million Jews would have had some place to go. We were trapped, and no country, including the United States, would rescue us. I have read many books about the Holocaust and Israel, and my children are also big readers and history buffs like me. We have a long history, the Jewish people – look what we brought to the world! The ten commandments are the basis of democracy and all civilization. Christian values originate from Judaism. And yet, there is so much anti-Semitism in the world. It seems that anti-Semitism is never going to go away. So we must support Israel!

My wife and I have always been strong supporters of Israel. I have traveled with my wife numerous times to Israel since getting married, and after that with our children. Israel is close to the heart of everyone in my family. I really believe that Israel is the future of Judaism. I plan on going again in the future with my children, If I am able to.

My wife and I have a lot of Jewish pride, which we instilled in our children. My wife may have been a more modern woman, but, she would never miss candle lighting on Friday night, and she wouldn't eat non-kosher food as long as I knew her. My son and my grandson both married converts who are so sincere and proud of being Jewish, keeping kosher homes, and like my wife, not eating in non-kosher restaurants.

When my wife and I bought a house, the first thing I wanted to know was about the synagogue nearby, before I would even buy the house. I was looking for an Orthodox congregation, because I grew up that way. I was always very active in synagogue, and at the time of this writing, in my late nineties, I still am!

My feelings towards G-d – that's a very tough subject, and not one I'm going to tackle in these pages. That's a private matter, between G-d and myself. I could have been angry at G-d, but anger can eat you up if you walk around angry all the time. I'm not going to live that kind of life.

I was five inches from death. Why did G-d save me?

I have no idea.

I've always talked openly about the Holocaust. My children and grandson Aaron know a lot about it, and they are knowledgeable, dedicated traditional Jews. It was my son Jeff's idea for me to write this book. I suppose there will come a time when his future grandchildren will not know me (I am, after all, 97 years of age as of this writing). So I agreed to put my memories to paper, so that when I'm gone, my descendants will forever know the story of my life, and of my family.

I asked my children and grandchildren to never forget where they came from. Their lives are miraculous; my survival was a miracle. I hope they will continue to love and support Israel, and be proud Jews for many generations to come.

Map Legend

(Numbers on map denote timeline of events from Fall 1942 through Summer 1947)

1. Oct 1942 I was taken from my hometown Sighet by the Hungarian army for slave labor and to Tasned.

2. In January 1943 I was sent to Budapest where I was housed in the city Zoo with other slave laborers.

3. In April 1943 I was taken as a POW by the Germans and sent to Ciuk (Satmar region).

4. In Fall of 1944 I escaped, making my way back to Sighet in October of 1944.

5. In November 1944 I was taken as a Russian POW and sent to Galicia.

6. In December 1944 I was sent to Donetsk. I worked on a coal mine here until the Spring of 1946, when I was sent to a collective farm 100 miles outside of Donetsk. In the Fall of 1946 I was sent to a different POW camp in the area.

7. In 1947 I was released by the Russians and returned to Sighet, stopping in Yasi along the way.

8. In June of 1947, I arrived back in Sighet. Shortly thereafter I would begin my journey smuggling myself to Germany, passing through Hungary and Czechoslovakia.

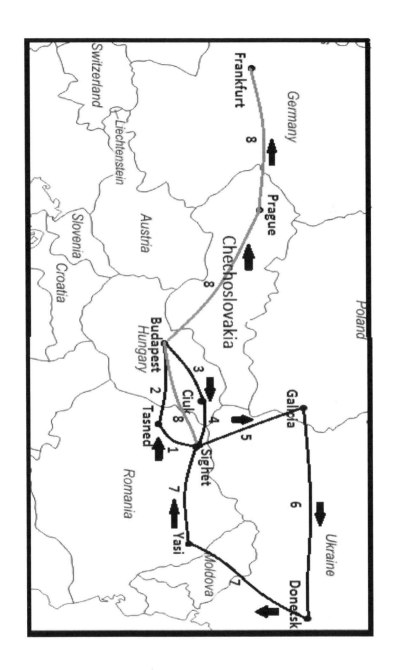

Chapter One: Family of Origin

My birth

I was born Dec 29, 1918, in Sighet, Romania to a large family of two amazing parents and eight children. In my childhood, Sighet had a community of 10,000 Jews, one half of the total population of Sighet. In my day, there was no such thing as "Reform" or "Conservative" Jewry. All of the Jews in Sighet were Orthodox, to one degree or another.[1]

---

[1] Most people in town kept the Sabbath and kosher. Most of the men wore a hat. The range of Orthodox practices in town ran the spectrum from more modern to very frum.

I was there to witness Sighet coming under Hungarian control in World War II, but as a child, I knew it as being in Romania.

There are few Jewish families who lived in Europe during World War II who can make this statement. Of the eight children in our family, seven of us survived, helped enormously by the fact that two of the children were already living in America when the war began.

Since many Jewish families were wiped out in their entirety, this fortuitous outcome is not something I take for granted. Still, I suffered plenty of loss from the murderous Nazis, especially the gassing of my beloved parents, one sister and her two beautiful children, aunts, uncles, nieces, nephews, and cousins. I would also say that the ordeals of the holocaust significantly impacted the well being of my surviving siblings. So although they did survive the war, they were forever changed, and thus, so was my family and I.

Before I share my personal story of survival and redemption, I wish to honor my parents, of blessed memory, with whom I was fortunate to have spent the first 24 years of my life. I am confident that much of who I am today, (the good parts anyway), are a credit to the home my parents created and the positive way they raised me. Here I am, privileged to live into my mid-nineties in excellent health, while the Nazis murdered my parents. My father was only 60, and my mother 58. They were robbed of the right to live a natural and long life as I have been privileged to do.

My parents married young, in a traditional religious marriage that came about through a matchmaker, which was the norm then. I always knew them to have a peaceful loving union, and an excellent partnership. Their solid model of shalom and love served me well when I later became a husband and father myself, with my beloved wife Rose of blessed memory.

My father

My Father, whom I called Tatty, Jacob (Yaakov) Mendel Davidovitch, a'h, was the kind of man who seemed to love everybody. In World War I, he was a soldier in the Austria-

Hungarian army. He was of medium height, a very quiet pious businessman, who worked most hours of the day in his business. But, his true love besides his family was learning Talmud and Gemara, which began in his childhood days in yeshiva. Father followed the *Visnitz Rebbe*, and he was certainly the most religious member of our household, wearing a *bekeshe*, a *streimel* and a religious beard. The *Rebbe* had a brother who lived in our town, and if my father had any religious questions, he brought them to this *Rebbe*.

When I say my father was very involved in the *Visnitz Chassidic shul*, that doesn't say enough. Not only was he the *Gabbai*, but also, he and another man really ran everything in *shul*, which was a sizeable synagogue with 200 built-in-seats. There was no Rabbi – 40 different *shuls* in town consulted with one chief Rabbi in Sighet. Our *shul* ran without a President or Board of Directors - whatever was needed, my father and this other man did it. The *shul* was what we refer to in America as "lay led." If the caretaker needed something, he notified my father for advice. He gave out the *aliyahs* (honors). He did it all. My father was a religious man who always prayed twice a day and whatever spare time he had after running his business and taking care of our large family was given to the *shul*.

One aspect of my father that I really appreciated was his tolerance for the religious differences in our family, which couldn't have been easy for him. My Hebrew teachers told my father that I would be a good candidate for yeshiva, and thus my father and I would talk from time to time about my learning. After attending yeshiva for two years, I started to deviate from the strict Orthodox practices of my father. I didn't pray at night, only in the morning. I didn't go to *mikvah* every day like my father did without fail. I didn't wear *yarmulke* – I wore a cap with visor, and I kept my *peyos* short. I was still the most religiously observant of the children, but compared to my father, I was not as stringent. Still, he never demanded that his children practice Judaism the way that he did. He understood that as a whole, the children are often different than the parents, and he didn't pressure me to be like him. I may have been less observant than he was of the laws, but he instilled in me a deep appreciation of being Jewish, and a respect for the traditions. I don't wear a black hat or a beard now, but of all the siblings, I ended up the most traditional. I think that's in part because my father let me find my own path and he didn't pressure me to be Jewish in exactly the same way he was.

Although my father was flexible about some Jewish matters, there was one absolute that he never wavered on: Shabbos dinner, Friday night, was a commandment in our household. G-d forbid one of us didn't show up for it! To my father, Sabbath family time was sacred, and I have to say, I looked forward to it, so I had no complaints. In the middle of the Shabbos meal, my father would sing *zemiros*, and I still hear his voice as I sing *Shalom Alechim* with family on Shabbos. Till this day, I have a great love of Shabbos. I am active in my synagogue and I even conduct the *shacharis* service, and sometimes *mussaf* as well. I enjoy very much our weekly *shabbosim* with my son and daughter, daughter-in-law and the grandchildren. I too, like my father, would not ever want to miss one.

My father was very busy with his business, and you can appreciate why. He was responsible for providing the means for a family of ten, and he didn't inherit a family business or any wealth. He had to build his own business, and it never came easy for him. His business manufactured and sold the fabric used for the Romanian peasants to make their heavy woolen clothes that protected them from the elements of the harsh mountain winters. He ran a small factory in Sighet that employed ten people. He also operated a storefront in the middle of town where my mother and some of the older siblings sometimes assisted him.

My father traveled a good amount by railroad for his business, shopping for raw materials.[2] He closed the store between 1- 3, as was the law of the land. When he came home, my mother served the main meal of the day. Even this weekday meal had a certain degree of formality to it, with a set table of nice dishes, and a formal tablecloth.

One experience I had as a young boy, in 1929, left a big impression on me. The big Depression that we are familiar with in America also rippled across the world into Europe as

---

[2] As we came closer to World War II, he couldn't travel because his beard invited anti-Semitic violence against him, so I took over and traveled for him.

well. It strongly impacted my father's business. He worked a whole year to build up inventory. The first time I ever saw my father cry was one day in 1929 when his customers, who normally bought wholesale from him in August, didn't have the money to pay him. He was wiped out and had ten mouths to feed. I heard him crying, "I lost everything!" The following year, he was forced to sell his inventory to wholesalers for half price. Even then, if they didn't have the money to pay for goods, they sent them back. He had to close the factory in 1930 and 1931 until he had sold off the built-up inventory. My father had a wealthy backer, a Jewish man with no children, Mr. Herman Stober, from whom he borrowed money to be able to keep the business from folding, and to live on, during this very hard time. He also relied on some financial support from my older sister Regina in America, which I'm sure must have been very embarrassing for him.

Besides the overwhelming responsibility of providing for a family of ten, my father also felt responsible to all of the workers in his factory who were counting on his wages to feed their own families. When I became a businessman myself, employing workers in my own factory, I never forgot witnessing the stress on my father from this ordeal.

Eventually, the Hungarians forced my father to close the factory. As a Jewish owned business, he was no longer able to secure any raw materials for his business.

My mother

My mother, Rachel ne' Zola, a'h, whom we called "Mommy" was a full-time housewife with her hands full caring for eight children. She never went to school past the 8th grade in the village of *Vad* where she was raised. But you would never know it – she was a very effective manager of our busy household. My uncle, who was educated and very close to her, called her "my lawyer." Many people came to her for advice, especially our relatives. Somehow she also managed to keep all of us from fighting with one another and we lived harmoniously, in a small house, with a lot of kids. (Trust me, I don't know if we'd see the same results in today's generation, in the more luxurious setting of America).

A short stout woman, she dressed as a conservative religious woman with her hair covered by a kerchief except when she went to temple, and then she wore a hat over a wig. She was actually pregnant ten times – two babies did not survive – and yet, I always remember my mother in full gear, with no downtime, pregnancy or not. I remember my mother as a warm, affectionate person who managed to make every child in our family feel loved and cared for. I've even been told the story of my mother's strength when my father was drafted into the army during World War I. In those years, when fathers were conscripted into the army, the family was left to fend for themselves. My mother was left with no *parnussa* (income), and four children to feed. She rose to the challenge by stuffing geese and selling goose liver, until my father returned from the army and resumed his business.

Like all of the Jewish women in our town, (even the ones without a lot of money), my mother employed young peasant girls to help us with the wash, and ironing. They slept near the brick stove in the kitchen. Their parents were not far away and they would go home to their families from time to time. Without modern appliances, it took days to wash and hang out the laundry to dry. With no washing machines, our clothing was most often washed in big pots that cooked on the stove. In the wintertime, they then carried it up to our attic to dry. Another peasant woman would then iron them once dry. Outside when the weather was miserable, it was no easy task to hang the clothing to dry – sometimes all of the wet laundry had to be *schlepped* up to the attic to dry over about four days. How much we take for granted the convenience of the modern washing machine!

It was a whole job for my mother just to make fire. My father bought firewood in the spring, and dried it over the summer. Then woodchoppers would chop it down to the size we needed, and we piled it into the wood shed. My mother cooked her food in a wood burning stove with an oven. There was a platform on top of it where she rested her pots.[3]

---

[3] There were also potbelly stoves in the bedrooms to heat up the rooms in our cold winters.

My tireless mother cooked three meals a day, every day, (except on Shabbos of course) with no running water in the house. Imagine the effort involved in carrying water in from a well. There were no drains so she had to remove the used water in buckets and bring it outside when we were done using it!

Producing the enormous amount of food we ingested every day, enough for a small hotel, was a big job. We had no car, so she walked to the market every day and bought fresh veggies and eggs. There was no chicken already cut, and wrapped in cellophane. It was my mother who would buy live chickens and bring them to the *shochet* to be slaughtered, unless one of the children helped her. She made homemade bread just about every day, including flatbread for breakfast. We often ate homemade soup, and a great variety of healthy food created from the fresh vegetables my mother purchased every day at the market or from our garden. My mother was a great cook!

We didn't own our own cow, so we bought milk from the farmer down the road, and one of us watched the milking to make sure it was kosher. Then my mother had to boil the milk because it wasn't pasteurized. She made delicious crème out of the skin. She received ice delivery every day to keep the milk and other perishables cold. On days when the ice wasn't available, she lowered the food in a basket with a rope and dropped it deep into the well.

For Shabbos my mother prepared what we consider in America a traditional Shabbos dinner. On Shabbos day we ate homemade *gefilte* fish my mother produced from chopping up fresh fish, and *cholent*, made from beans, barley, meat, and marrow bones, which we picked up from the bakery where our cholent pot baked through the night. (My siblings and I would fight over who had to retrieve the pot from the bakery!) After the chicken was slaughtered, my mother would turn that chicken into delicious Friday night chicken soup, and Shabbos day chicken. She also made *tsimmes* (carrot pudding), potato kugel, and always, her own homemade challah.

My mother was a pious woman who prayed in shul every Shabbos before Rosh Chodesh, even though it wasn't standard practice for the women to go to shul more often than the High Holidays.

My grandfather

My father's parents, and my mother's mother, were deceased before I was born. *Zeidy*, my mother's father, was the only grandparent I ever had the opportunity to know. He was known as "Reb Yossel" to the community. His official name was Joseph Zola, and I called him *Zeidy*. We believe his family originated from Spain and was chased out by the Spanish Inquisition, and eventually settled in Hungary. He owned the town saloon in *Vad*, which was closed on Shabbos. This commitment for a saloon that was pretty remarkable. It was located in the village where my mother was raised. Like my father, he was very learned in Gemara and well respected in his shul. He was a true *talmid chochim*. He gave a *shiur* (lesson) every Shabbos in his *shul*. He sported a long white beard and very much looked the part of a *tzaddik*. He was the most religious member of our family. One of my best *Zeidy* childhood memories relates to Chanukah. A ritual he created for our family that centered around his gift to all of the children of a pile of Romanian coins, the height of which correlated to our age. *Zeidy* lived a good long life, until the age of 72, which is probably the equivalent of living until his nineties in this generation.

My siblings

My mother gave birth to two siblings who did not survive, and I do not know their names, or the circumstances of their death. I had seven living siblings, and here is a recording of what happened to each of them.

My oldest sister **Regina Zola** was quite a bit older than the rest of us, born in 1905. As a young boy I was always running behind Reggie to give her the "latest news". When she got tired of listening she pushed me out the door! She left Sighet in 1928, to America to get married to my mother's brother, Morris Zola. Because she was living already in America, she escaped the holocaust altogether. It was very hard on my mother to let her go so far away. But, they kept in touch with letters exchanged in Yiddish. We didn't see her for five years, until she returned to Sighet to attend my sister Shari's wedding. Reggie and Morris had one daughter, Evelyn, who married Leonard Kassel and became Evelyn Zola Kassel. They have one son, Jonathan Kassel.

My next older sister was **Charna** (everyone called her Shari), born in 1907. She was a beautiful young woman who married Shlomo Fructher who was in the lumber business and lived in another town of Satmar. Reggie's visit for Shari's wedding was the first time we got a chance to meet her daughter, Evelyn. Shari and Shlomo later had two children, Heddy and Yossi, ages 10 and 6. Shari and her children were murdered in the gas chambers. She was the only child of my parents who was gassed. Shlomo survived, remarried, and moved to Israel.

Frida, (whom we called Frimmet), was born in 1913. I remember her as being sweet and kind of quiet. She married Ari Hanz, from a small village in Czechoslovakia, on the day that the war broke out in the USA (Pearl Harbor Day). By then, in 1941, the war was going on, and their wedding was a simple affair. A few months after they got married, Ari was forced into Hungarian forced labor. She returned home to us, and then Frida got deported with my parents to Auschwitz with Pepsci (Joan) and Lilly. Ari and Frida both survived the war, and they settled near Prague. They have one son, Bobby Hanz, who married Florence, an Israeli girl who died young of cancer. He has two daughters, and four grandchildren, and lives in Brooklyn. Bobby served two tours of duty in Vietnam.

Born after three girls, in 1914, my oldest brother, **Louie's** bris was surely a much- celebrated occasion! I learned a lot from Louie as my older brother. We called him Libi. As a teenager, he got involved in a Zionist organization, *Misrachi*, and in 1936, he decided to move to Palestine (what was later to become Israel). He could not have known that he would never see my parents again, who were very upset when he left. He got sick with malaria in Palestine, and had a lot of trouble with the Arab riots, so he only stayed there two years. In 1938, he immigrated to America to join my sister, Reggie. He signed up to serve in the American army, even though he wasn't a citizen, and then served as a mechanic with General Patton's army corp.

After the war, Louie returned to America and Pepsci (Joan) matched him up with a friend of hers, Etu (Loretta), a girl she went to school with in Sighet. They had two children, Harvey and Ronnie. Harvey was married and has a son, Etan. Ronnie was married also and has a daughter named Rebecca. Every Rosh Hashana and Passover, Harvey comes to stay by me. He lives now in Fort Meyers, Florida, about 200 miles from me.

Four years later, in 1918, I was born.

Two years after my birth, the fifth child was born, my sister **Joan**, named for my father's mother, whom we called by her Hebrew name, Pessel, or "Pepcsi" for short. She was born on of all days – 9-11, in 1920. Joan had a strong personality. We were close in age and teased each other like typical siblings. She was deported to Auschwitz with Frida, Lilly, Shari, and my parents. She survived, and lived a long life until passing only within the last year at age 94. She was widowed from Michael Ferencz, and her children, Gerry and Karen, grandchildren, and great grandchild were her pride and joy. She lived most of her life in Queens and Westchester, N.Y.

My younger sister **Lilly** was born two years after Pepsci in 1922, and she and Pespci were very close. I always remember Lilly to be very neat and clean. She loved to polish my shoes for which I gave her a coin! She married William Schneider and they had two children after the war, Renee and Shari. Renee is married to Shelly Palmer, a lawyer, and they live in New York City and the Hamptons. Shari has a son, Paul. Lilly lives now in an assisted living facility in Queens. I speak to Renee from time to time to see how Lilly is doing.

Moishe, the baby of the family (who took the name Eddie in America years later), was born in 1923. Being the baby of the family he was pampered by my mother. He has had a very hard life. He survived forced labor and was then imprisoned in the concentration camp *Mauthausen* in Austria. He barely survived, and returned to our home suffering terribly from typhus, lice infestation, and severe depression. Moishe eventually married Pearl, and they had two children, Robin and Jeffrey. Tragically, he has suffered the loss of his wife and both children. Fortunately, he has two grandchildren, Paul and Samantha, from Jeff and his wife Sue. He also has a great grandchild, Jackson! Moishe lives in an excellent assisted living facility in Commack, NY. I speak with him several times a week and periodically visit. His daughter-in-law, Sue Zola, is like a daughter to him and she takes care of him very well.

Chapter Two: Childhood

My schooling and friendships

We lived near Transylvania, in Northwest Romania, in a valley surrounded by the beautiful, majestic Carpathian Mountains, with the *Iza* and *Tiza* Rivers flowing on the edge of our town. It was beautiful country and a far cry from the landscape of my current home in Florida. I had a lot of friends as a child, and although I was one of many children, I didn't hang out with my siblings very much, except for sometimes my older brother, Louie.

I attended a public school, and beginning at age 5, also attended early morning and afternoon *cheder* for my Hebrew studies. I rose at 6 AM and attended cheder until 8 AM. Then I returned home, ate breakfast, and went to school. My public school was a mix of Jews and non-Jews, and I learned there until 2 PM when we went home for the afternoon meal. After our mid-day meal, I returned to *cheder* and learned there until 8 PM at night from a very Orthodox Rabbi (we called him a *malamed*) with a long beard. I would return home from *cheder* and do my homework, falling asleep at the table.

Some people might think that *cheder* was the equivalent of what most Jews in America call "Hebrew School" but believe me, it was much more demanding than that. We didn't get a summer vacation – we learned in *cheder* the entire year, except for the month of *Tishrei* and a week off for *Pesach*. On *Simchas Torah*, as soon as the holiday was over, the Rabbi called out, "Okay boys, back to *cheder*!" Even on Shabbos afternoons we would learn *Pirkei Avos*.

We didn't know from school busses – we always walked to school, no matter the weather, and sometimes it was very cold. In Sighet, there were maybe 2 cars in a town of 25,000 people. We could hire a horse and buggy, (we didn't own one ourselves) but as a kid, I walked everywhere. In

America, it seems that everyone feels the need to get into their car to go wherever they want to go. I still preferred walking when I could, when I was younger.

Shabbos and the Jewish Holidays

Shabbos was an important ritual for our family, especially my father, who was more Orthodox than the rest of us. Jewish stores dominated the main street of Sighet. We purchased only kosher groceries from a shop run by a religious man and his wife, the Lisers. We set the Shabbos table with our best china, and my mother dressed very elegantly in a kerchief or a hat. She lit candles in a big candelabra that sat on our dining room table. Only my father and the boys went to *shul*, and when we came home, my father made *Kiddush*. He often brought home *yeshiva students* from shul to eat the Friday night meal with us. These same *students* would eat weekday meals with us as well.

In the wintertime, with snow on the ground, Shabbos days were short. In the spring or summer, on Shabbos afternoon,

I got together with friends, hanging out on a friend's farm with lots of trees and teenagers hanging around the orchard while my parents napped. After napping, my father sat on our wraparound porch learning the Talmud. When I was younger, and my grandfather was alive, he would often test me on whatever I was learning.

We didn't have the convenience of indoor plumbing and electricity, so we used kerosene lamps and candles! On Shabbos night, once the candles burned out, we were sitting in the dark, or talking with our friends by moonlight. During the day we depended on light through the windows, and as the end of Shabbos neared, it got very dark in the house until we could light the lamps again. At the close of Shabbos, my father insisted that all of the children be home for the *Havdalah* service that ends the Sabbath. As we grew into teens, some of my siblings did not want to come home from being with their friends, and eventually, my father permitted them to miss *Havdalah*. I was not so rebellious and was generally there.

As I mentioned earlier when discussing my parents in Chapter One, attendance at Shabbos meals was commanded, and for the most part I enjoyed them. My mother's gefilte fish, chicken soup, stuffed cabbage, kugel, and compote were always delicious, and I appreciated the Shabbos atmosphere in our home.

Jewish holidays in our town were very festive. Practically all of the business people in town were Jewish and 99 percent of the stores were closed. You couldn't buy a needle on the Shabbos or holidays. Everyone walked to shul and home. We met our friends on the streets. It was a lot of fun, especially because most of the Jews in town were participating.

Rosh Hashana was our most important holiday. It began with *Slichos*, for which we got up at 4:30 AM, for the week prior to *Rosh Hashana*. *Rosh Hashana* was very solemn. We all went to *shul,* including my mother and sisters. The women had a separate entrance into the balcony, with windows to look down to the men. We didn't have a permanent Cantor or a Rabbi – just a *baal tefillah* who was a member of the shul. I remember he was very good! Someone blew the *shofar* in the shul. Like in America, we dipped apples and challah into honey, and my mother served up her famous Hungarian goulash and stuffed cabbage at our *Rosh Hashana seuda* (meal).

My father wore his kittle on *Yom Kippur* and I fasted as soon as I reached *bar mitzvah*. We broke the fast at home. Because my mother was in shul all day on *Yom Kippur*, and she wasn't in the house to warm up the food. I remember breaking the fast on cake while waiting for the wood stove to warm up the chicken soup.

I helped my father build our *sukkah* out of wooden two by fours, with walls made out of a straw material, which we decorated with a kind of carpet on the walls that the peasants made. Our *schach* was made of pine branches. The girls hung decorations from the ceiling. My father ate in the *sukkah* no matter what the weather, but he didn't sleep there. The *sukkah* was big enough to fit the kitchen table and except for when the weather was poor, we all ate in the sukkah together. To my father's credit, he never demanded that I, or my brothers, join him for the breakfast meal if the weather was particularly cold or wet.

Sometimes we'd see snow by *Simchas Torah*, but it never stopped us from celebrating because for this holiday we were inside. *Simchas Torah* a joyous celebration that included dancing with the Torah and *hakofas*, but not the candy apples we see in today's shuls!

For *Chanukah*, my father lit the *menorah*, and we visited Rebbe Hager, the Borsa Rebbe who had a large following in town of at least 1000 Jews. We played *dreidel*, and visited my grandfather to receive our *Chanukah gelt*. We feasted on our share of delicious Chanukah latkes. We didn't know about donuts!

I remember delivering *mishloach manos* (cakes and sweets) for *Purim* with my brother, Louie and making money from tips. My mother and her friends made the kind of fancy delicious cakes you can still find in some Jewish bakeries today. I might have tried wearing a costume once or twice, but I didn't go for it. My father gave out money to the poor who came begging, and we enjoyed a family *Purim seudah* (meal) with my mother's delicious *kreplach* (dumplings) for the soup made from sautéed chicken and onion. I don't remember the men drinking. I never saw my father drunk. I do remember watching a few *Purim* plays but never acting in one myself.

You haven't seen cleaning unless you witnessed the way we cleaned our home for Passover! "Are you going to clean the roof too?" a Christian neighbor asked us. We started a few weeks before the *Yom Tov*, and hired help to wash everything! We scrubbed and scrubbed, including the walls. Even washing the floors for Passover was a project because we had to bring water from the well in buckets. We laid out all of the books on tables outside of the house, looking through every page for a single crumb – which of course we never found! My father went through every corner of the house the night before with a feather and candle, looking for a missed crumb.

The good part about Passover is that it was the one time of year I got a new suit and a new pair of shoes. For a boy in my town, if your shoes or suit didn't last during the year, you had to make due until Passover. So by then, I was eager for a new suit, having often outgrown my previous one. I remember my father coming into the house with piles of shoeboxes that he bought for all of the children and also for he and my mother, in one of his shopping trips out of town. If the shoe mostly fit, it was good enough! We brought the Passover dishes down from the attic, beautiful dishes, and my mother and sisters set a fancy *seder* table. It seemed as if my mother was cooking for Passover for many days. She baked special Passover cakes, and we enjoyed matzoh balls instead of noodles for our chicken soup. Until then, we ate special Passover noodles, made out of potato starch and eggs. (It's delicious – I made it for Passover in America for many years. My kids love it!). She prepared special Passover gefilte fish, which she kept cold in our water well, and my father would pull it up with ropes when it was ready to eat. We also ate *shmura matzoh* made in the town kosher bakery dedicated only to matzoh baking. Contrary to American practice of latkes being a Chanukah food, we enjoyed them a great deal over Passover as well. We didn't have any processed foods from the supermarket for Passover – we ate a lot of potatoes and eggs!

I don't remember loving the Passover *seder* itself — it dragged out, and I often fell asleep when I was very young. Still, it was an important ritual in our family's life and one that I have treasured as a father and grandfather.

On *Shavuous*, in the springtime, all the *shuls* in Sighet were beautifully decorated in greenery, and the sweet aroma of walnut branches and leaves filled the air. My mother made delicious dairy meals, especially her renowned dairy coffee cake, and we celebrated receiving the Torah with many festivities.

Going away to yeshiva

In contrast to my sisters, as a boy in a religious household, everything changed for me when I became a *bar mitzvah*. Caterers who wanted to drum up business started the whole big *bar mitzvah* celebration in America. In my day, when you were a *bar mitzvah*, they called you up to the Torah, you celebrated with a small *Kiddish* in the house, and that was it - no big deal. My father bought me a black hat but I didn't wear it too much. After my *bar mitzvah*, I was sent away to yeshiva.

I was the only son of three boys to be sent away to yeshiva, because I had the capacity to learn *Talmud* and it was important to my father. Yeshiva was no fun, let me tell you. It was about a four-hour railroad trip away from home, so I only came home a few times a year for the holidays. Our learning day began at 5 AM. The Rabbi who ran the yeshiva tested us every Saturday afternoon. We were kept busy learning every day, all day, and into the night. I went to yeshiva at age 14, and by age 16, I had had enough. I came home and told my father: "I'm not going back to yeshiva anymore." He accepted my decision and put me to work in his store instead.

In the next chapter, I share the beginnings of war coming to our town. We saw clouds gathering when Hitler came to power. Looking back into my childhood, I see that there was always an undercurrent of anti-Semitism in school, like being called "dirty Jew", or the non-Jewish students being jealous of Jewish students performing well in school. The Jewish students stuck together and didn't really have anything to do with the non-Jewish students. We only socialized amongst our own. Still, we managed to co-exist until the *anti-Semitic* tension in town rose to new levels.

Chapter Three: Early War Years, 1939 - 1943

In 1939, in an ominous sign of more trouble to come, police officers started checking our identification. One had to carry ID wherever one went. If you didn't carry ID, and you were stopped, arrest and detention were likely. Never mind that the arresting officer might have just been in our store as a customer and knew full well who you were. He didn't even pay for his purchases! Once in detention, bribes were required to pull strings for release.

Fortunately, I always carried this big piece of paper that was my identification, so they never took me in. In Sighet where we lived, the police and local government were corrupt. There wasn't one Jewish policeman or any Jew holding public office in the city or state government, even with a fifty percent Jewish population. Without bribery money, you couldn't get anything done.

By August, **1939,** we knew that war was brewing. I traveled to the Romanian capital, Bucharest, hoping that I could get an American visa from the consulate. When I got there, they told me I needed more documents and I wasn't able to get my visa. I returned to my family on August 31, 1939. On September 1, 1939, Hitler attacked Poland.

With anti-Semitism rapidly spreading through the area, it wasn't safe for my father to travel with his beard and orthodox garb. Since I had no beard or peyos, and I didn't wear a black hat, I traveled for my father until we lost the business.

In 1940, Sighet came under Hungarian control. Our area, Transylvania, was a disputed area before the First World War, when it was under the Austro Hungarian empire. When that empire disintegrated, Romania took control. But in 1940, Hungary wanted back their territory, so they struck a deal with Hitler. He cut Transylvania in half – half went to the Romanians, and the other half returned to the Hungarians. He wanted both Hungary and Romania to be his allies in World War II.

Our lives became miserable under Hungarian rule. The Hungarian regime took away most of our rights, but at least they didn't deport us to our deaths. Hungarian Jews did not feel the heavy sting from Hitler until 1944.

Once the Hungarian army and police took over, they acted as if they owned everything in Sighet. An army officer even took a room in our house. We had to give it to him, no choice. We became a closer family, sleeping four of us in one bedroom, to accommodate him. Actually, once we gave up a room, the army kept sending different officers to sleep in it.

In 1940, the Hungarian government cut off all Jewish-owned businesses from access to raw materials for goods, so my father was essentially put out of business. His factory couldn't get raw materials to manufacture wool yarn and fabric. He kept the retail store open, by buying in the markets different homemade materials to sell. I often traveled for him to help keep the store stocked. Mostly, we got by on our savings, and from the materials we had left in the store.

My parents were born in Transylvania when it was part of Hungary. Because it had become part of Romania after WWI, they now had to prove that they were Hungarian citizens. This was despite the fact that my father served as a soldier in the Hungarian army in the First World War! In the US if you have a birth certificate showing that you are born in America, you are an American citizen. But my father was harassed for one paper or another, traveling to Budapest, the Hungarian capital, to prove his citizenship. Many Jews were harassed, and deported to Galicia, Poland, where the Germans and Russians were fighting, if they couldn't prove they were Hungarian citizens. Tragically, hundreds, if not thousands of Jews were shot in Galicia by German S.S. They lined up the Jews, made them dig their own graves, and then after shooting them dead, complained about needing to wash Jewish blood off their hands and shoes, when they crossed the border back into Hungary. They were animals.

My parents were eventually able to prove their citizenship, only to be gassed by the Nazis some months later, in May 1944.

The Hungarian government – was undoubtedly antisemetic but you could survive there until the mass deportations in May and June of 1944, when outside of Budapest the country was "ethnically cleansed". They came out with all kinds of anti Jewish laws. Hungarians don't operate under the bribery system. If they have a law, they enforce it, no matter what. An example of a law they instituted was ownership of a radio. (We used to listen to reports about what was happening in the world on BBC radio, which ran broadcasts in 70 languages and we would listen when they spoke in Hungarian or Romanian). The Hungarians went as far as forcing all of the Jewish homes to turn in their radios. Other Hungarian laws included no relations between Jews and Christians (sexual relations and intermarriage between them were illegal). All goods were rationed, and the

Hungarians made sure that the Jews didn't end up with ration cards. It seemed like every week there was a new law against us.

While the vast majority of Jews did not realize the horror that was coming, my father was more knowledgeable than most. He went regularly to shul, where people talked about what they knew. Polish Jews escaped, crossed the border into Hungary, and found their way to the synagogue. They reported on the situation that had developed in Poland and the danger to the Jews.

In 1941, the Nazis attacked Russia, and the German army went through my town to fight Russia. Then, the anti-Jewish laws really escalated, because the Hungarian Regent (like a King) of Hungary was a terrible anti-Semite. Initially, the German army didn't stay in Sighet. We saw them riding through in the railroads, but we were still under Hungarian rule. At this time, I am 23-years old, and mostly focused on helping my father continue to manage the store and bring in parnussa (a living) for our family.

In the Summer of 1942, the family store was stolen from my father. I wasn't there to witness this, but I heard about it from my father. A Hungarian civilian from Budapest walked into the store sometime after Transylvania was divided and Hungarian occupation was established. He simply declared, "I like this store, and I want it. Jews have no property rights. There's not much merchandise, but it's a good location on the main street, close to other stores, and across the street from the courthouse.". My father had no choice but to watch this Hungarian peasant steal his store. He gave my father only one day to vacate. There wasn't much merchandise left at that point. From then on, our family had to rely on savings, and selling leftover inventory from his factory, and merchandise we had left in the warehouse.

My days of Hungarian slavery

In 1942, when I was 24-years old, I was conscripted into Hungarian slave working battalions. Not just me – a couple thousand Jewish men were drafted into the army from my town if you were considered "of military age," age 20 – mid 30s. Most of my friends were conscripted at the same time.

I'll tell you – at the time it seemed like a bad thing, but in retrospect, if not for this event I probably wouldn't be here to give this testimony. When the Nazis deported my family to concentration camps, I wasn't home. Forced labor with the army was for me, a very lucky turn of events, as hard as it was.

I remember the exact day I was summoned because it was on *Simchas Torah 1942* when I received a summons in the mail to present myself to an army building. They loaded us on the trains, and transported us to this half-finished army building in the town of *Tasned.* They conscripted young Jewish men from all over the region for forced labor, so I was with Jewish men from towns all over, not just Sighet.

Toilet facilities were located a half-mile away in the mud from our sleeping quarters. The building had no windows or doors, and no beds – we slept on straw placed on the cold cement floor and it was freezing. We brought blankets from home. They made us rise at 6 AM, and we stood on line to be counted and for a cup of fake coffee. (Real coffee was a delicacy then, imported from South America, and it was too expensive to import for us!) They gave us subsistence food just to keep alive. Till this day I don't eat lentils. They gave us lentil soup every day and it was black, along with dried string beans that tasted like barbed wire. Thankfully, my family was home still and whenever they could, they sent me some food. My married sister, Shari, lived not far from there, so sometimes she came by the gate, and was able to get precious items through for me, like an extra blanket and socks, and food, because the officer at the gate liked her.

Hungarian sergeants and officers in uniform were our commanders. If your commander had a heart, was a human being, you got along. If he was a beast anti-Semite, he would give you a lot of trouble. I was lucky. I had a man over me who was pretty reasonable. He was an older man, a retired schoolteacher, with rank of lieutenant. He was company commander. One sergeant was impossible, but I got him good. I was tired of trudging through the mud to use the facility, so I got myself a jar and put it at the end of where I was sleeping. In the middle of my night, I voided into this jar. This sergeant came in drunk, saw the jar, thought it was booze, and took a good swig, almost finishing it. Boy did he carry on when he realized what was in that bottle! I denied that it was mine and in the morning, I got rid of that jar.

We wore our own clothing, and later on yellow arm bands were required, worn over our sleeves to label that we were Jews.

I was in Tasned from October 1942 until January, 1943. This ironically was the town where I had gone to Yeshiva for two years. This town was about one hour by rail from Satmar, where my sister Shari was living.

We went out to work every day doing manual labor that included snow removal from roads and digging antitank ditches. They held us there for when we might be needed. In January 1943 they loaded us up in trains and cattle cars. None of us knew where we were going. There were all kinds of rumors. Were we going to the front in Poland? Thankfully, no. They moved us to Budapest and house us in the zoo, minus the animals. It wasn't so bad. We were not mistreated on a relative scale. We were able to leave and go into the city for personal items, food and so forth. This situation was the luck of the draw, under the command of the kind lieutenant. We were on the edge of the main thoroughfare. The rest of the winter 1943 was spent in residence at the zoo. We slept on straw in barns, without heat but adequately nourished.

We spent the rest of winter 1943 removing the snow from tracks at the station. It felt like they were keeping us busy, just to give us something to do, waiting for the real work to come in the future. These Hungarians had to show the Germans that they were extracting labor from the Jews.

I was in Budapest January through March.

In April 1943, they made us march to the train station, and put us in cattle cars; we traveled on this train for two days. Once again none of us knew where we were going. They didn't stuff us in like sardines. They provided us with salami, bread and water. We were not treated as badly as the Jews who were deported and gassed. We had heard of Dachau from before the war and were frightened of transfer to a concentration camp, although at the time we had no knowledge of Auschwitz. They took us to the Romanian border, in a region called *Ciuk*. We were there the whole summer, living in barns, building roads and digging holes for telephone poles. We had to climb up the poles and put in the accessories for the wires. It was dangerous, heavy, exhausting work. Daily we worked as long as there was light, installing miles and miles of poles all over the mountain. Some of the overseer soldiers were brutal and cruel, hitting us with sticks, and some were humane. Fortunately, my unit didn't suffer any serious injury.

At this point, the Nazis had not yet deported my family. I wrote my father a letter, explaining to him that after a year and a half of service, I was eligible to apply to come home. He saved my life by advising me, "Stay where you are; do not come home". He knew what was coming. My father had a cousin living near the Hungarian-Polish boarder who had given my father reports of atrocities in Poland. Mass executions on the Polish side were being perpetrated, with the killers trying to clean the blood from their hands at the cousin's house. My father was not in denial like many Hungarian Jews were.

While we were in Ciuk we used to visit a Jewish widow who cooked kosher food in a tiny restaurant, and her chicken soup, chicken, and potato latkes, were a great comfort to us. In 1944 the Nazis deported her and killed her, like all the other Jews. All the while we were in the army, we were afraid that they would take us too to the concentration camps. We never knew from one day to the next what would happen to us, or our families.

We worked six days a week. Sundays was a day off. But we were the lucky ones.

In August of 1944, Romania turned against the Nazis. King Michael arrested Antonescu the dictator, who cooperated with the Germans. The Romanian government became allied with the Russians who had overrun the country. The war had taken a very ugly turn for Hungarian Jews. The German army, battalions and battalions of them, flooded the area I was stationed in, by the border of Romania. As the Germans occupied Hungary, they rounded up the Jews and deported them to ghettos, and ultimately to their deaths.

In 1944 I became an orphan. And my life in the army got a whole lot harder. We continue this part of my journey in the next chapter.

Chapter Four: 1944

1944 was the worst year of my life.

I was still under the control of the Hungarian army, moving from place to place. For two years, I didn't sleep in a bed. We slept in barns at night, and we supplemented our diets with food from the land around us. In the mountains, we competed with the bears for berries. Food wasn't plentiful but we were young, and we could survive these conditions, as miserable as they were.

Now we were working in the mountains, installing telephone lines. We had no shelter from the cold, snowy weather. So, we cleared away the snow, and cut branches from the trees to make huts. We lit a fire and spent the night in these primitive conditions.

Yes, I lost my freedom and the comfort of home, but I had nothing really to complain about compared to what happened to Hungarian Jews, including my family. They were still in their homes around Passover, 1944, when the Germans occupied Hungary. Special units of the SS were assigned to round up all the Jews into ghettos and then deport them to Auschwitz.

First, the Jews were crowded into the ghetto. This happened more than 70 years ago, but I remember it like yesterday. I got a postcard from my mother, and she wrote, "We are going away from the house, to a new life. Hopefully we will be all right and I plan to write you where we are". All of the Jews were told to write this.

I know now, that by the time I got that postcard, she, and my father, and one of my sisters, Shari, and her two darling children, were already gassed. (The same devoted sister who visited me with extra food, blankets, and socks).

Thankfully, my oldest sister Regina and my older brother Louis, were already in the States. My father, mother, and three sisters, Frida, Joan, and Lilly, were forced into the ghetto. My younger brother Eddie was in slave labor under control of the army, although he and I were never together. Maybe my family could have saved themselves. We had a Romanian domestic who begged them, "Come, I have a cabin in the mountains, no one will bother you there." I think my family did not know about Auschwitz, and didn't realize how much danger they truly were in.

In May 1944, they shoved my dear family into cattle cars, 50- 60 in one car, with no food or water, no air, and no room to sit. I still have nightmares thinking about how they suffered. My sisters told me, my father was begging for water, "a little water, a little water." My poor father never got his much-needed water.

I was still serving under the Hungarian army while all of this was going on. The monster Mengele sent my father, my mother, and my sister Shari with her two beautiful children to their death right away. Three of my other sisters were also there for a year. Together, Frida, Joan, and Lilly all survived Auschwitz along with the death march that forced them to walk for days in the snow without food or water. My surviving sisters are a miracle. Only a very small percentage survived Auschwitz and out of them only 50% made it thought the death march. It is also very rare for three sisters to survive together, but they protected and watched over each other the whole time. When they came off the train, in Auschwitz , Mengele sent one of my sisters, Frida, to her death, but Joan was very courageous and acted very quickly. When the guard looked away for a quick second, she pulled Frida back into the line going to work, instead of to the gas chamber.

So you see, when I think about what my family suffered, I can't complain about my wartime army experience at all.

Back to my story, which was no fun at all, believe me, but it's all relative –

In 1944, we were in Hungary very close to the Romanian border. The Romanian government became allied with the Russians. As the Russians crossed the border into Romania the Germans had to clear out. The Hungarian army started to retreat with the Germans, and they took us along. I'll never forget one particular night in Hungary: We were retreating and were running in a downpour. It was September 1944. The sky just opened up. In the middle of this unbelievable torrential downpour my commander said to 100 of us: "Stop!" He took us all into an empty courtyard. No one was there. The whole population of the town had run away, afraid of the Germans. They made us stand in this yard in the pouring rain the rest of the night. In the morning, they turned us over to a German officer.

I was sure this was the end.

They took us to a German compound around 10 AM. A German officer asked us, "Who speaks German?" My mother always told me, '*Stay hidden; don't volunteer unless you must. Let them not know you.*' I followed her advice and kept quiet. Another guy replied that he spoke German. So he translated for us.

The German officer said: 'You are going to carry ammunition for us up this mountain' which he pointed at.' Anyone who tries to escape will be shot'. They gave us each a crate of ammunition. That crate felt like 200 pounds. There was absolutely no way to carry it – there were no good handles. and we were supposed to walk it up a mountain. It was impossible. We improvised handles made out of branches and roots, and two of us carried two crates stacked. German soldiers with machine guns surrounded us with their fingers on the trigger. *One wrong move, we were dead.*

It was so hard to climb the mountain with this ammunition. We walked ten minutes, sweating top to bottom, then they let us rest for five minutes or we would pass out. On the way up, we met SS officers, the Gestapo coming down the mountain. They asked our overseer: "Who are they?" He replied, "They are Hungarian Jews." He said, "Bring them up there and get rid of them." We understood it was their intention to shoot us dead once we got to the top of the mountain. We had no choice but to continue up the mountain, really in agony.

We left the bottom of the mountain at 1 PM. Seven hours later, at 8 PM it was dark, and we had finally reached the top. The commander said, "Put down what you are carrying. Sit down."

I waited for the end. But unbelievably, they did not kill us. When we reached the top, bullets were flying all over the place, with the Russians and Germans shooting at each other. We sat down, waiting for the machine gun fire that would kill us. We were terrified, didn't know what would be in the next minute but nothing happened to us!

Then they told us to go back down the mountain. That took us about three hours, and by the time we reached the base of the mountain, it was about 1 AM. We slept at the bottom of the mountain in a barn, after they fed us some food. The next day, the Germans told us to return to the top of the mountain, to bring the ammunition back down, because the

Russians had broken through, and the Germans were retreating. This was just crazy. I hid from the commander and did not go back up that mountain again. There was just no way I was going to go through that nightmare again.

The Germans were now retreating, afraid of the Russians, and they took us along. They stole cattle from the peasants, town to town. We Jews were responsible for the cattle. One time, we came into a house that still had food on the table. Most of the population of that town was ethnic German and they fled because they were afraid the Russians would kill them. The whole city was empty. As we went through each town, I witnessed the German army burning these towns to the ground. They bombed the railroads and left total destruction in their path.

The Germans took us up to a battlefield to carry away wounded soldiers who had been hurt in the mountains. There was a railroad at the bottom of the mountain and the idea was that we would put the wounded soldiers on these trains. But every one of them was dead! We were walking along a ledge with a 500 foot drop, in the dark, so the walking was really rough. Another time, the Germans pushed the Russians back a few hundred yards, and both sides were shooting at each other. We were caught in the middle of it all.

One morning, after a battle in which the Russians retreated, weapons were left behind. They took ten of us into the valley where there was fighting, to pick up stray weapons. I looked around and spotted a pair of *tefillin* left there, probably from a Russian Jewish soldier. A German guard grabbed it and put it to his ear; thinking it was a secret communication device and he sent it up to the intelligence office to examine it more closely. He didn't ask me what it was, and I didn't volunteer any information. That was my motto: *keep your mouth shut.* That helped me a lot.

Another time, we were working hard, carrying ammunition. I laid down on the grass during a lull and fell asleep. All of a sudden, I woke up to a terrible pain, like someone shot me in the back. I was screaming, "I'm hit." *I really thought I was dying.* A German soldier took me to the battalion doctor who examined me. Turns out I was hit by shrapnel, which, by the way, may still be in my back, because it went in but never left. So the doctor gave orders that I shouldn't walk, and I had to be carried in the horse and wagon. I faked it for more than it was, milking my injury for a couple of weeks to get out of all the walking.

We were retreating, going west, and we were still far from Germany. We traveled about 30 – 35 miles a day, so this injury turned out to be very lucky for me and it got me out of miles of walking.

By now, it was September 1944, and we were exhausted. When we got to villages, I would lie down outdoors, and sometimes wake up in a puddle of water. One night, I slept in a barn near big German horses – Clydesdales, and I fell asleep behind a horse's hind legs. I woke up to the horse stepping on me!

One day, we passed a town that used to have Jews living there. I knew this town. I said to my two friends, Krindler and Linder, "Let them shoot me. Whatever happens, happens. I'm not going anymore! They are taking us further and further west. All they are going to do when we get to

Germany is put us into concentration camps anyway. That's it, I'm deserting at my first opportunity!"

There was always a German soldier behind us and he got tired because that day, we were walking 50 – 60 kilometers. He went into a wagon, so there was no soldier behind us. We were each herding cows and I hit my cow very hard so it would run into the fields. I made believe I was running after the cow, but I never came back. My two friends did the same trick and they followed me.

We made our way back into town. As far as I know, the soldiers didn't even see us leave. In this town, by coincidence, we found our old Hungarian outfit, the guys who originally handed us over to the Germans. The officer asked us, "What are you doing here?" I told him, "We ran away from the Germans." He warned me, "You can get shot for this." "Yes, I know, but I can get shot anywhere," I replied. This officer said, "You can stay with us, or leave, but I have no responsibility for you." He could have turned us over to the military police, but he didn't. Maybe he hated the Germans too.

We didn't want to join him, but we asked him to help us get some food. He told his cook to give us some bread and salami, and then we were on our own.

In the town of Bethlahem, we had to hide before the Russians advanced. The whole town was crawling with Hungarian and German soldiers. I knew if any of them caught us we were dead. We found an empty house with no furniture, but mezuzahs on the door. They had a barn with an attic full of hay. We crawled into the barn and went to sleep in the hay.

We were exhausted and slept the whole night. In the morning, we heard someone climbing the ladder up to the hay loft where we were sleeping; We were really scared that we would be discovered. It was a Romanian peasant that found us in there. He pointed to a fence and said, "Be quiet. I know who you are. Soldiers are coming for the hay and they will catch you. I'll tell you what to do. Over that fence is a Jewish cemetery. Climb over the fence and hide in the cemetery, no one will bother you there." This man hated the Germans and the Hungarians, so he wanted to help us. We listened to his advice.

We were hiding out in the cemetery and a Romanian peasant threw boiled potatoes over the fence for us. My father and I dealt with Romanian peasants, and we always got along with them. It was now October 1944 and it got cold at night. All I was wearing was a pair of pants, a torn shirt, and a bad pair of shoes. One of the guys with us, Linder, was a heavyset guy, and he couldn't exist on these boiled potatoes. He said to us, "I'm too hungry – I'm going to look for food." I said to him, "If you go out, you'll get a bullet!"

He went out and never came back.

So then it was just my friend Krindler and myself. We couldn't sleep outside without warmer clothes, so at night, we decided we would crawl back to the barn, but we heard soldiers' voices in the barn and crawled away on our hands and knees without being seen. We found a haystack about

200 feet away to hide in; it was soft and warm and we slept there the entire night. No one came looking for us.

In the morning, we came out, and all was quiet. It seemed as if everyone had left the town. We were going to go back to the cemetery when we came to the fence and I heard Russian soldiers all over the place. I understood Russian and I heard the commanders telling their own soldiers: "Go Go Go!" It seemed that the Russians had occupied the town.

I wasn't scared of the Russians – I figured they were our liberators, our friends. So Krindler and I walked out into the street, expecting this to be a day to celebrate. Instead, a Russian soldier grabbed my friend, who was wearing Hungarian military pants, hit him in the head with a gun, and shoved him into a lineup of Hungarians to be shot in the street. An old gypsy woman who spoke Russian told the sergeant holding a Tommy Gun "This guy is a Jew; he didn't fight against you. He is your friend." The Russian soldier waved his right hand and told my friend to get out of the line. He then mowed down the line of prisoners. She saved his life.

Then a Russian patrol brought us into headquarters. We found a Jewish officer who spoke Yiddish, so we told him our story. He was a Soviet Jew, and he asked us, "Where are you from?" He took out a map and we showed him. We asked him how we could get back to Sighet. He said, "Wait here three or four days and your town will be liberated."

While we were waiting we befriended Russian soldiers who were very friendly to us and we drank vodka together. We found empty Jewish homes to sleep in. Two days later, my friend and I realized that the only way we were going to make it back to Sighet was to walk – more than 200 miles – because there was absolutely no transportation. The whole region was devastated.

We started to walk and then an unbelievable thing happened to us. As we were walking, a Russian army patrol stopped us and ordered my friend and I to work, fixing the roads! We were free one minute and prisoners again the next. We did this for a day, and then we learned our lesson. They let us go, and from then on, we walked by the rivers and fields so that the army wouldn't pick us up to work. We slept in barns and along the way Romanian peasants gave us food.

We walked for two weeks. On the way we picked up a farmer, a Jewish fellow who was walking home to a village on the outskirts of Sighet. By the time we got to his farm, someone had harvested all of his corn. He pleaded with us, "Stay here, see what will happen, don't go." But I told him, "I have to see what happened to my family." We stayed in his house overnight, but then left him and walked about 7 miles to Sighet. I was still with Krindler, whose family was also from Sighet.

Arriving in Sighet: October, 23, 1944

The first thing I did when I finally arrived in Sighet was to go straight to my house. I found Hungarians living there. I recognized them. They used to live across the courtyard from us. They thought no one would ever be coming back, so they just moved into our house. I told them, "I don't want to make trouble. I'm just looking for what is left, like my clothes. I have nothing." They let me into the house and I looked for something to wear but all of my clothes were gone. I changed into a suit of my younger brother's, and a pair of shoes that belonged to him but didn't fit me. Christian neighbors welcomed me back home and gave me another pair of shoes that fit me better, and I found a coat in the house that belonged to me. I had nothing else. I was furious to see these Hungarians living in my parents' home, but I couldn't say anything, because I was afraid to rock the boat.

A former housekeeper, Maria, saw me in the street and invited me to stay in her cabin, in the mountains but I declined. She was the same one who offered refuge to my parents, but they declined. She's the one who told me that she had tried to save my parents from deportation. She was in our house since I was little. She really helped raise all of us children. In the streets, I saw some Jewish people drifting back, and coming out of hiding because the Nazis were gone and the Russians were in charge. I saw some people I knew, but no one from my family.

The first night in town, I slept in my maternal aunt Gittle's house. (Someone was living there, but there was an empty bedroom and they permitted me to sleep there). The next morning, I heard that a friend of mine had returned home, Kaufman, so I went to see him. Eventually, there were at least 10 friends and acquaintances who survived, all gathered together. I never could have predicted what was to come next. In comes a Russian officer with his patrol, and they stationed themselves by the doors and windows. I saw right away there was trouble. He spoke Romanian and asked us, 'Do you want to fight Hitler? The war is not over yet. There is a Chezch legion being formed to fight and looking for volunteers.'

"Yes!" We responded.

Hitler had killed my parents. I had lost my home, and I was fighting mad. What did I have to lose? I agreed to join the legion to fight. He took me and several other guys escorted by Russian soldiers to a prisoner of war camp outside of the city.

Yes, that's right. A prisoner of war camp!

Can you imagine?

This turned out to be the biggest disappointment of my life.

I thought I was free already. I had started to make plans for the future. But here I was back in a lice-infested prisoner of war camp. I later found out that the Russian commander of the town had a Hungarian girlfriend. She told him, "the Jews are coming back. They are robbing the people, and they want their houses back." He sent out the patrol to pick up every Jew they could find, and in my area, they rounded up approximately 80 of us.

I fell into the trap. The rest of the Jews hid once the word got out that the Russians were capturing the Jews.

I was out of my mind and I had no one to speak with about this. I tried to explain, "I am not your enemy. I want you to win the war." No one would listen. After the second or third day I spoke to one of the captains. I knew these Russians loved watches and cameras, they were like God to them. I had a German *Leica* Camera I had hidden before the war and it was very valuable. So, I told him, "If you let me out I will give you the camera". Of course he agreed to this. He took me out to town and I went to find the camera, buried in the backyard of my home. I gave it to him, but he didn't honor his word and took me back to the prisoner of war camp!

This was a new low for me.

After two weeks, they started marching us northeast towards Russia. We walked, and walked, and walked. I couldn't stand it and I was always looking for a way to run away. One day, in a split second, I took my chances. We were turning a corner and I ran into a courtyard, hiding. Ukrainians were there, and they ratted on me, and the Russians came after me with their guns. I was just lucky. I was running so fast into the formation they didn't shoot me. But they caught up with me and I was captured once again!

By this time, it was the end of November, 1944 and we were freezing. They weren't feeding us, and many of us were getting sick with all kinds of diseases. I was very afraid of contracting typhus. They took us to another camp in Galicia, Poland. Once again, they treated us like we were the Germans, their enemy. That camp was full of mud, barracks with bricked over windows, and barbed wire. One day, the Russians formed a transport into Russia. I could have stayed in that awful camp, but, I was afraid of getting sick. So, I agreed to go on the transport to Russia.

They boarded us on cattle cars going East, and eventually to Sachta in Donesk, Ukraine near the Russian border. Several thousand of us packed into 40 or 50 cattle cars. They put a stove in the center of the car, and a place for going to the bathroom. But the stove had no coal to warm it. The only food they gave us was salty fish and no water. People were dropping like flies. The Russian Commander was taking a head count every day. He was going to deliver us to the Russians, dead or alive.

There was a doctor on the transport, a woman who counted the dead every morning by banging on the side of the cattle car calling out, "how many dead do you have this morning?" Russian soldiers stole prisoner's shoes if they liked them. Everyone knew life in Russia without a pair of shoes in the wintertime would be a death sentence. Luckily they didn't take mine.

We were in that God-awful train for two weeks! We arrived in Donetsk on December 15, 1944 in the evening. When we arrived I could barely walk. The wind was howling, and I was frozen stiff. Somehow I got my legs to move from the train station to an empty building that had nothing in it but bunk beds. There was nothing else there. I took my shoes off and slept with them under my head to prevent theft.

When I woke up the next morning the guy sleeping next to me was dead. The ground was so frozen that we couldn't even bury the dead. We had no choice but to stack the bodies outside, frozen together until the spring thaw. The guys around me undressed the corpses for clothing.

We were hundreds of men; Jewish, Romanian, and German, all prisoners of war mixed together. In the mornings, they gave us a piece of bread, and some tobacco. Stupid people, some of them came to me and traded their food for my tobacco. Those men didn't survive. But, I was happy to trade my tobacco for the bread.

We were in this prison camp for a few days. Soon after, about 200 of us including all the Jews were relocated to another camp in the area where at least it was warm, and we had plank bunks to sleep on. Relatively speaking, it was a better situation, but it was still no good. At least this camp had heat, and they deloused us. It also had a kitchen, albeit a terrible kitchen, but it was something at least. One day, I saw a lot of supplies coming into the kitchen, like meat and flour. We got our hopes up, thinking; maybe it will be good now. It turned out, they were just fooling the Red Cross that came in for an inspection. As soon as the Red Cross left, they took all the food away and we existed mostly on sandy cooked potato peels.

Friends of mine were dying, either from starvation, or because their bodies could not withstand the illnesses they were contracting. I guess I had a stronger constitution luckily. I was very skinny, but I was not sick. Nonetheless, my spirits were very low and I was very angry.

One minute I had been a free man, and now I was a prisoner again!

My Father Jacob Mendel Davidovich during World War I as a
soldier of the Austro-Hungarian Army.

My Grandfather Joseph Zola and his second wife,
their daughter in the middle, and my sister Regina
on the right.

My Mother Rachel Zola Davidovich.

My Father Jacob Mendel Davidovich.

From Left to Right: My sisters Shari, Joan with Lilly below her, my mother, Frida standing, my father holding my brother Moshe (Eddie) , and myself standing with Louie sitting below.

My brother Louie on the left, unknown child, my sister
Regina, and myself on the right.

My mother with my sisters Regina on the Left and Shari on
the Right.

From Left to Right: My sisters Frida, Regina, Shari, and a
Romanian peasant girl at our drinking well.

(Above) Moshe (Eddie) with my sisters Lilly on the left and Joan on the Right at the family well.

(Below) My sister Frida.

My sister Joan strolling through Sighet.

Evelyn, my sister Regina's daughter, along with my brother
Moshe (Eddie), during her visit from America for my sister
Shari's Wedding.

My sister Shari holding Evelyn and my sister Regina holding unknown child on the right.

My sister Shari, her husband Shlomo, and their beautiful
daughter Heddy.

My sister's Lilly (left), Joan (Right), and niece
Heddy.

Shari and Shlomo's son Yossi above with their daughter
Heddy below. Shari, Heddy, and Yossi all perished at
Auschwitz.

Jewish Organization membership card shortly after coming
back to West Germany from Russia.

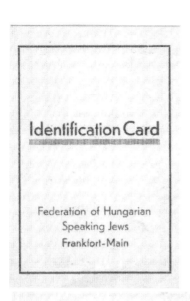

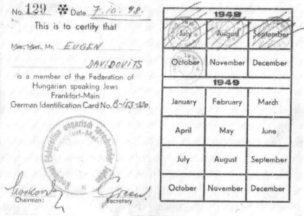

Membership card to the Federation of Hungarian speaking
Jews in Frankfurt.

West German Identification card.

EMBARKATION CARD 28
Einschiffungskarte

S/S   MARINE MARLIN

Sailing-Date: JAN 1 0 1949

Accommodation   B 20 - 15
Schiffsplatz

Mr.
Mrs.   DAVIDOVITSCH
Miss   Eugene

Hans Henfe, Bremen, Heidelberg 200

My embarkation ticket on the S/S Marin Marlin from Germany to the USA in 1949.

Restitution application denial upon arriving to the USA in
1950 from Hessische Minister in Frankfurt.

My wife Rose and I, 1950.

Our wedding day, January 6, 1951.

My beloved wife Rose.

At my son Jeff's Bar Mitzvah

Standing from left to right: Bobby (Frida's son), Harvey (Louie and Loretta's son), unknown woman, Louie, Loretta, Mickey, and Joan.

Seated from left to right: Renee (Lilly and Willy's daughter), unknown man, Evelyn (Regina and Morris' daughter), and friends of the family.

Back row left to right: Stanley, Jeanette (Rose' baby sister), Yetta (Rose' older sister)
Sitting: Abe, Tessie (my father and mother in law), myself, and Rose.

Standing: Second from right my siter Regina with Eddie third from right. Sitting: Morris, Willie and Lilly (my sister), Pearl (Eddie's wife), and his sister in law.

My Daughter Shelley

In my card store in Manhattan.

Plaque from our work at the Jewish Federation, 1982.

Plaques I received from the time I spent as Chairman of the Rockwood Park Jewish Center.

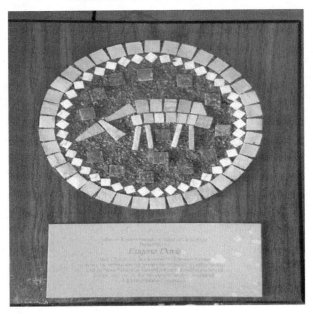

Rose,my grandson Aaron, and I in 1986.

Above my grandchildren Alexis, and Aaron holding Laura.
Below my grandson Steven.

IN LOVING MEMORY OF THE

DAVIDOVITZ FAMILY

FATHER: YAKOV MENAHEM B. 1884
MOTHER: RACHEL NEE ZOLA B. 1885
SISTER: CHARNA & CHILDREN
YOSEPH & CHANA
OF SIGHET, RUMANIA
MURDERED IN AUSCHWITZ, MAY 1944

DEDICATED BY
EUGENE, EDDIE & LOUIS DAVIS
JOAN FERENZ, LILY SCHNEIDER, USA

Our family's memorial plaque at Yad Vashem, the holocaust Museum in Jerusalem.

At the Passover table with Rose at Shelley's house.

Rose and I at my granddaughter Alexis' Bat Mitzvah.

Rose, my grandson Steven, Shelley, Art, and me at Steven's Bar Mitzvah.

My grandson Steven, my brother Eddie, and me.

From left to right: Myself, Joan, Lilly, and Eddie at a family
reunion.

From left to right. My daughter Shelley, my wife Rose, myself, my son Jeff and Susan at my grandsons Bar Mitzvah.

From left to right: (top) My son Jeff with his wife Susan,
grandchildren Alexis and Steven beside my daughter Shelley and
her husband Art. (below) My grandson Aaron with my wife Rose
and me holding granddaughter Laura.

Chapter 5: 1945- 1947

1945

I was in the burying detail for a few days before I was ordered into one of the worst jobs of my life. I was placed in a unit going to the coal mines. The Russians treated me like a Nazi. That was the hardest thing of all. Stronger people than me didn't make it. I made up my mind that I was going to survive this; *I must survive it, I must survive it.* That's what I kept telling myself.

We were working in the Russian coal mines. I don't wish that horror even on my enemies. Modern mines lower you down the ground in an elevator, but we went down and up a long ladder, maybe 100 slats. We had to climb down and up this ladder in the dark holding a lantern at the same time. It was always damp down there, and we breathed in the coal dust all day long, with no masks to protect us. The

Russian foreman gave each of us a pick ax, to remove the coal out of the wall.

We did this miserable job for 8 hours a day for what seemed like an eternity.

We filled metal railroad wagons with coal, and one day, one of the wagons got loose. I tried to stop it and I broke my right wrist. It hurt like the dickens, but we had no medical attention there. If you went to their so-called "infirmary", all you got was a treatment called "cupping." I had no choice but to put a rag around my wrist and keep on working.[4] The only good thing about working in the mines was that most of us tried to steal away a hunk of coal to make it warmer where we slept. We could only do that when we were working in a mine that had an elevator- otherwise we couldn't carry the coal on the ladder. Sometimes we got away with it, but most of the time the Russian guards took the coal from us for themselves, when we went into formation to go back to the camp. The Russians needed to get warm too!

---

[4] I never did get medical treatment for my broken wrist, and till this day, one of my wrists is thicker than the other.

One day, they took us to a section of the mine that I had a very bad feeling about. I said to the guys with me, "this part of the mine isn't shored up, it's going to collapse." I told the Russian foreman, but he ordered us to stay in the mine. I said to him, "shoot me – I'm not staying here!" I urged the guys to go with me and we got out of that part of the mine fast. Ten seconds later, the whole section collapsed. If I hadn't followed my instincts, I would have been just another casualty of the war.

Conditions in the Russian labor camp were brutal. We scarcely slept, and when we did, we had bedbugs crawling all over us.

Around mid-January 1945 they took us to work shoveling coal into freight cars. The temperature felt like 20 degrees below freezing!
Anyway, I just didn't know how I would survive the frigid Ukrainian winter. After work detail one day I went to another barracks to check on a friend of mine from Sighet. In that barrack I noticed two locked doors in a corridor, one with a Romanian peering through a small window. I asked him what he was doing there. He said that I should go away, because they were all in isolation and that they were all

contagious. He said that they all had scabies. So, I asked him if they had to work and if they had food. I found out that they didn't have to work and of course they were fed. Also, they were given medication to apply to their skin. So, I thought fast. Maybe this is not such a bad thing. I told him to let me in there! At first he said "no". Luckily, I had some tobacco on me. I offered it to him if he would let me in. So, he agreed and after one day I started to itch! I didn't apply the medication and I got to spend the rest of the winter inside. In the Spring, after using the salve, the scabies cleared and I was released from isolation. I returned back to the barracks and to shoveling coal.

One day in May of 1945, there were five of us Jews speaking Yiddish in the latrine. A Russian officer by the name of *Varza*, said to us in Yiddish, "What are you doing here? You don't belong here!" We told him our story and he said, "I will see what I can do to make it easier for you". Since we all spoke Yiddish, it was clear that we were all Jews. He was a political officer(Politruk), a member of the Communist Party, and he had more power than the camp commanding general. He told us he was from *Beserabia* (today known as Moldavia), and that the Nazis had killed his whole family.

There were about sixty of us Jews, and he took most of us to separate quarters. He gave us straw mattresses instead of the boards we had been sleeping on, clean clothes, and blankets. He gave us the best news ever; which was "from now on you aren't going into the mines. You will stand by the entrance and supervise the others". We guarded the formation when they went to the mines – we didn't walk with them in the formation, but rather, we walked on the side as if we were soldiers. We carried big sticks, specially made, in case someone deserted. We also got better rations.

This guy helped me survive. One day he asked me in Yiddish, "how come you are so skinny?" I was only about 100 pounds. He said, "Come with me." He took me into the kitchen, and told the cook: "whenever he comes for food, you give it to him." Food? I couldn't believe my luck. This guy had a *yiddishe* heart. Before this guy took care of me, I was living on so-called potato soup made from dirty potato peels.

I took advantage of his offer and started to rebuild my strength and put back some of the pounds I had lost. I was still skinny, but at least now I had a shot at not starving to death.

1946

One day a Russian commission of army officers and doctors showed up at our labor camp in the summer, looking for run down and skinny men who were too sick and malnourished to work anymore. Lucky me, I qualified to go home! I was too weak and skinny to work anymore. Also, I was registered as a Romanian, and in Romania there was already a communist government. I was a citizen of an ally of theirs.

My freedom was so close I could taste it. They approved me to go home. I was about to get on the transport to go home, waiting by the gate for the truck to come pick me up, and instead a Russian officer appears. He rounded me and five other guys up and told us we had to work on a collective farm 100 miles away. Can you believe it? I was a prisoner with no rights, and again I couldn't say anything! Who am I going to talk back to? They could kill me! There were no laws – these officers could do whatever they wanted to do. I wanted to survive so I caved in and went along with it, but inside, I was screaming.

We were in this collective farm for about five months, through the summer of 1946 and into the Fall. We were starving. We literally ate worms from the ground, and we grew some melons and ate them when they became ripe.

One day, they sent me to the fields to work with hay. I became friendly with a German prisoner. One day he said to me in German, "Let's go into a village and get some food." It was quite a long walk. We didn't run into any guards, so it seemed safe. The Ukrainians and Germans had just been through a big war, and the Germans devastated the Ukrainians. I told him, "Let's go to a house and tell them we are Jews and ask for food." The first house we went to, I told them I was a Jew, and the homeowner slammed the door on me and gave us nothing. So the next house, we decided to tell them that we were both German and they gave us some food! It was so surprising to me – these Ukrainian people hated the Jews but still preferred the Germans even after they had devastated their towns! We returned to the collective farm – we had no choice. But at least I had some food in my belly.

1946- 1947

In the Fall, they moved me to another prisoner of war camp and held on to me for another 8 months. Now I no longer had the Jewish officer advocating for me, and I had no one to talk to about my plight. A lot of the Jews who were with me didn't make it. If you got sick and didn't have the right medication, you were dead. In the area where we were stuck, there were pieces of wilted cabbage lying on the ground from the neighboring fields. We were warned not to eat it, or we might get dysentery. Some of my comrades were so hungry they ignored the warnings and ate the cabbage anyway. Sadly, many of them died from severe dysentery. I never touched this cabbage.

One day, while I was standing in formation I got dizzy and passed out. They took me to the infirmary, where I was delirious from a high fever of 103 degrees. I begged the orderly, "please give me a cold wet towel." I really thought I was going to die. He did me a favor, and gave me the towel, and eventually my fever broke; that towel saved me.

Even though I was on death's door, I fought to live. There was no use getting depressed or angry, or giving up. I had family in America and I dreamed of someday immigrating to America and putting this whole nightmare behind me. I recovered in the infirmary, and while I was there, I swore to G-d, *I will get out of this*. I could see people getting sick because they were starving, and eating foul food off the ground. Word was going around not to drink the water, and those who did ended up with bad diarrhea. But you had to drink something to stay alive, and after awhile I got immune to it.

Finally, they discovered on their records that I had been sent home, but I was still there! In the Spring of 1947, I got word that I'm going home. Once again, I was told that a truck was coming to the gate to take me to the railroad station. Just like a bad déjà vu movie, as I'm getting ready to get on this truck, an officer comes along and tries to take me back to work. But this time I was lucky. A Russian doctor who was on the commission that was supposed to send me home, just happened to be by the gate, and witnessed the scene. He said to the officer, "Let him go. You can't take him. He's going home."

Unbelievable. It was finally happening. I was on the train, headed home. I was rail thin and sick, and beaten down from three years of imprisonment. But they didn't kill me, and I had a second chance at life, which millions of Jews didn't get.

I was 29-years old. The Germans, and then the Russians, stole away my twenties, all of it. I couldn't complain – I was still alive – and this is a lesson for everyone. No matter what the danger, no matter what tight situation you are in, don't lose hope. Don't give up. If you give up, you are finished.

I never gave up hope, and now I had a chance to build a good life for myself.

They put me on a truck along with some other guys who looked as bad as I did, and dropped us off at the train station in *Sachte*, Ukraine. I had nothing with me, just the shoes on my feet, and no train ticket. Luckily the train conductor could see that we were prisoners and he didn't demand payment. We traveled west, crossing the border into Romania and headed to the city, *Yasi*. Before the war, there was a significant Jewish community there so, I, and a couple of other Jewish guys set out to try to find any remaining Jews. We asked around, and found a synagogue. We slept there, and some nice Jewish people gave us food, and some cash.

We stayed there only one night, and then took a train to *Satumare*, sitting on the floor because we had no tickets.

Before the war, I had a sister Shari living in *Satumare* with two children, but they all went to Auschwitz. I also had a Jewish friend from childhood living there, Appel. When I arrived in *Satumare*, I went in search of him and found his apartment. I knocked on the door. When he saw me, he cried. I asked him, "Can I take a bath here?" He gave me clean clothes and took me to a place to get eyeglasses, which I hadn't had in a long time, and he also gave me some money. I was very greatful as you can imagine! He was now married, but had no children. I stayed with him for two days, and then it was time to return to my hometown, *Sighet.* I had to find out exactly what happened to my parents and family.

It was June of 1947 when I arrived in *Sighet*, but I didn't stay there. I went right away to my sister, Lilly, who lived fifty miles away, in *Borsa*, a village tucked away in the Carpathian Mountains on the outskirts of *Sighet*, where her husband Willy Schneider had a lumber business. She had no idea I was coming. The only thing she knew was that I had been dragged away to Russia! My sister was so happy to see me. She had married Willy only one year after the war and I had known Willy from before the war. I stayed with her, her husband, and their newborn daughter Renee for three months while I restored my health and put on some weight. During that time I went back and forth to *Sighet* a lot where I stayed with my best friend, Mendel Stern, who had survived and returned to Sighet. He and I spent a lot of time together, sharing our war stories. During that time, commuting back and forth between *Borsa* and *Sighet*, I saw the signs that the communists were taking over. The Russian army was there, and the Prime Minister was a Communist. I wanted to get out of there fast, before they captured me again and I'd never make it to America.

Fall 1947

I knew I couldn't stay in *Sighet* or near my sister Lilly permanently. Once I was strong enough to leave, I told her that I was headed to Germany, to the American occupied zone. I was very concerned about the government of Romania turning communist, and I didn't want to get stuck there. I told my sister and Willy to come with me, but Lilly was afraid that her baby would make noise and endanger all of us crossing the frontier between Romania and Hungary. I went to Satmar by rail with a friend and then we were driven to a spot, close to Hungarian border, where we walked across the Hungarian border, avoiding border patrols.

I decided that I was going to make my way to Frankfurt, Germany, where I had learned my younger brother Eddie was in a DP camp, near Frankfurt. He was communicating with Lilly after he left Sighet, perhaps in 1946. I hadn't seen him since 1943. At that time though, traveling was difficult, and refugees such as myself had to get around by smuggling ourselves across the border. What choice did I have? There was no way I could get a passport. As I said I left my sister and smuggled myself across three borders, on foot, across frontiers and by rail to cities – first to *Budapest*, Hungary, and then to *Prague*, Czechoslovakia and ultimately the American Zone in Germany. We had money for train tickets but before boarding we needed to clean up to avoid undue suspicion.

I traveled with two other guys, and we smuggled ourselves in the nighttime by walking across the border when the guards weren't present, or were distracted. Sometimes we paid a guide to take us the safest way. We hid behind trees, and sometimes walked as much as six miles in a single night with only natural light. After we made it into Hungary, we walked until we found a railroad station. It was September/October and we were all muddy. We didn't want to draw suspicion to ourselves on the train. We looked around and saw a paved area and some water where we could clean up as best we could. I used the money Lilly gave me to purchase train tickets to Budapest.

No one bothered me on the train to Budapest. I knew Budapest quite well because I was stationed there with the labor battalion in the zoo. I also traveled there on business before the war. They were allies of the Nazis but in the fall of 1947, when I was there again after the war, the Russian army was in Budapest. My friend, Mendel Stern in Sighet, told me to go to his cousin, whose name was also Mendel Stern, in Budapest. I went to him. My traveling friend and I separated, he stayed in Budapest. Stern was living with his wife. He told me, "You have to go to Czechoslovakia , closer to Germany. I have someone who wants to go with you. You speak Hungarian and he speaks Czech, so you can pass yourselves off as either nationality. The Hungarians spoke to us a few times on the train so this came in handy. We took a train to the Czech border, where we hired a guide and crossed the border on foot, and ended up in *Cosize*, Czechoslovakia.

We then got on a train to take us to Prague. I had notified my sister Frida that I was coming because she lived there. My oldest sister Regina, who was living in America, coincidentally was visiting Frida. She and her 19-year-old daughter Evelyn met me at the train-station in Prague. The last time we had seen each other was at my sister Shari's wedding in 1931. I parted from the guy I was traveling with, and I traveled with Regina to Frida's house in *Usti*, where she was living with her husband Armin, whom she married before the war, and now their three-month old son Bobby. In 1944, Armin volunteered for the anti-Nazi Czech Legion, and after the war, the Czech government provided him an apartment. This area was called *Sudetenland*, a region Hitler had conquered. After the war the Czechs expelled the ethnic Germans. They reclaimed the area for Czechoslovakia and took possession of the entire industrialized area. I didn't want to stay there, I was still afraid of the communists. My aim was to go to America, and from Usti I would never get there. I only stayed with my sister a week or so. Then I was on my way to Frankfurt, my best chance for getting to America.

Regina had a very big heart and she gave me a bunch of money to help me along until I could get to America. All in all, I managed to smuggle myself over four borders – Romania to Hungary to Czechoslovakia to Germany, and I was never caught!

In Czechoslovakia, in a town called *Ash* that was on the German border, there were Israeli agents who smuggled Jews to Israel. Traveling by myself, I went to a "safe house" there, where agents from Israel were operating. When I got to the house, the agent asked me if I wanted to go to Israel. I said "No, I want you to help me cross the border into Germany to see my brother." He agreed to help me just because I am a Jew. He invited me to sleep overnight, and then hid me and other Jews in an army truck covered by canvas, and took us across the border to the Munich Railroad Station.

The city was destroyed but the train station where I was dropped off was intact. I took the first train out of there, and I remember it taking most of the day. At that time, the German marc was so low, I could trade a dollar for 300 marcs. I paid for this train ride with dollars given to me from Regina.

Finally, I arrived in Frankfurt, Germany. For the first time I felt free, which is ironic since I was in Germany! None the less, in Germany I didn't have to run away from communism, and I felt protected by the American army that was there on occupation to "de-Nazify" the region, and to transform Nazi Germany mindset into democratic principles. Germany at that time was a country of about 80 million people. The Nuremberg Trials took place just a year before I got there. It would take a big effort to change the mindset of all of Germany, helping them shift from Nazism to democracy was no easy feat. The Americans were in charge until about 1950 – the German police were even under American rule. The steady presence of the American army helped reassure my fears.

My younger brother, Moshe (most people call him Eddie, which is the name he changed to when he came to America, but I still call him Moshe), who was at the DP camp, picked me up from the train station. I hadn't seen Moshe since 1943. I was elated to see him, as well as all of my surviving siblings. Moshe was living in the DP camp, *Bad Salzstlif*, which was about an hour train ride from Frankfurt. He was living with other guys in a section of Germany that was mostly bombed out. He took me to his DP camp in a fancy spa/hot springs, where rich people used to vacation. They had to put the refugees some place! He was sharing a room with another guy.

I only stayed with my brother a few days. Then I rented a room in Frankfurt, again, using money that Regina gave me, instead of staying in the DP camp. I exchanged her dollars into marcs and it went a long way. A German woman and her daughter rented me a room in their house with a separate entrance. At that time, if you talked to Germans, you couldn't find a single Nazi anywhere. This woman didn't have much and she needed the income, so I rented the room from her and it served me quite well. I was lucky to find it – Frankfurt was all bombed out and it was hard to find a room anywhere in the rubble. At that time, you could buy entire buildings for only $10,000, and those who did became very wealthy when Frankfurt was rebuilt. When I was there though, the ravages of war had basically destroyed Frankfurt.

I remained in Germany for a year, going back and forth between Frankfurt, and where my brother was, Munich, and all over Germany by railroad. I went visiting other DP camps, where other Jews were living to see who survived. At that time, there was hardly a single refugee who didn't get involved in the black market, and I was certainly one of them. This activity led me to one of the more memorable experiences of my time in Germany:

I was doing some black market business with my friend, Mendel Stern, who followed me to Frankfurt. He also had rented a room there. We noticed that the local butcher didn't have any meat to sell, because the supply was depleted by the war. The citizens of Germany were tightly rationed, maybe receiving as little as ¼ a pound of meat a person per week. Near the DP camp where Moshe was, were German farmers. I approached one and asked if he was willing to sell me a cow, an illegal venture. I then spoke to the local butcher: "If I got meat for you would you be willing to buy it?". His reply was a definite "yes".

I bought a cow, slaughtered by the farmer, about 25 miles away. Now, I had to get the meat to the butcher. I found a neighbor with a truck who I paid to bring the meat to a group of butchers who were eager to buy it. It was a profitable endeavor, but completely illegal and I could have gotten in big trouble for doing it. Fortunately, I got away with it. I did it a few times, and then stopped.

Besides this interesting "cow" business, I also sold coffee beans on the black market. At that time, a package of coffee beans, or cigarettes, was like gold. Louie who was in the US was about to get engaged. He sent me cigarettes and packages of green coffee beans, and I sold enough to buy a 1.5 carat diamond to send to him for the engagement ring! I sent him 15000 marks approximately $500! Smoking was so popular then, if you finished your cigarette and threw away the butt, someone behind you would pick up that butt and smoke it!

I was part of a community of thousands of Jewish refugees who took over hotels, and army barracks. Conditions for me there were not awful because I became part of a system, cared for in the DP camps, supported by American Jewish organizations, and given help by the JDC (Joint Distribution Committee). Displaced persons had privileges at that time. The German citizens stood in line for everything. If we had certain ID papers, we always went ahead of the line. Food was rationed. But, we got double rations and kosher food. They gave me an ID. After the war, Jews who survived the

Holocaust had a lot of doubts about religion and God. These Jewish organizations were paying a lot of attention to kosher and Shabbos, and trying to get Jews back to believing again. They took excellent care of us.

I spent my time mostly in the American occupation zone, waiting for my eventual immigration to America, and in the meanwhile, doing some business. A lot of single men like me were dating in the DP camp, and looking to get married, but it wasn't for me. I knew I was headed to America, and I wanted to figure out how to make a living before I committed myself to marriage. I told myself to wait (and of course I'm very glad I did!).

Moshe went ahead of me to America 8-9 months before. He went to our sister Regina and her husband Morris' apartment in the Bronx. Louie took over the apartment lease when Regina and Morris bought a house in Jamaica Estates, Queens. Joan was already living in Queens. Frida and her family were headed to Queens as well. I was looking forward to living in close proximity to family again.

Chapter 6: Immigrating to America

While I was in Frankfurt, President Truman proposed a law that Congress passed. It gave visa priority to homeless people, Jews included, to be allowed to immigrate to America in record numbers. Within three months, instead of waiting the usual time, which could have gone on for years, I registered under that law. In this way, I was able to immigrate to America in 1948. I was almost 30 years old when I came to America.

---

[5] So how did I get the last name Davis? It actually originated with my brother Louie. The army changed his name to Davis, because his commander couldn't pronounce his last name. When I met my wife, she couldn't pronounce my name either, so when I applied for citizenship in court in 1951 I officially made my name Eugene Davis.

We departed from a big port in Germany, *Bremenhafen* on a ship called the Marina Marlin, a Liberty Ship designed especially for transport of soldiers to Europe from America. I was registered as Eugene Davidovitch[5]. UNWRA(UN works and refugee agency) funded my voyage and thousands more.

It was a comfortable ship. I was one of about 500 refugees and one of the only few who didn't get seasick. The crossing took 10 days. I still have the boarding pass. You hear a lot of stories about refugees on harrowing boat trips, but because this boat was primarily used to transport soldiers to Europe, it was a much classier boat than most. We even had waiter service – I remember a black man wearing a black suit, with a towel over his arm, serving us three meals a day. It wasn't the Queen Mary, but the service was nice! What a contrast to what I had been through!

When I got off the ship on January 20, 1949, I was at Pier 42 in New York with ten dollars in my pocket. I brought some gifts through customs for my sister Regina. I had bought for her some nice Rosenthal plates and a handmade lace tablecloth. The custom agent said to me, "That will cost you ten dollars." I handed it to him and then I had nothing left in my pocket!

I was one of the lucky ones who had family already living in America, so I didn't have to enter the country as a refugee with no place to go.

I can't even describe the feelings I had when I first set foor on American soil!

I turned around and my brother in law, Morris Zola, was standing there. He took me to their house in a section of Queens, called Jamaica Estates. They were married in the late twenties, and their daughter, Evelyn, was living with them. My sister Joan had immigrated before me, and she was not yet married and was also living with Regina and Morris.

I spoke not a word of English. The culture shock of living in America when I scarcely spoke the language was very hard on me. My sister Regina was very smart. She saw me one morning reading the Yiddish newspaper. She took out the NY Times and handed it to me and told me to read that paper instead. I reacted with; "I don't know how to read English. I can't read this newspaper!" She responded, "You'll learn one word a day, and before you know it, you'll know how to read English."

She was right. I read the NY Times every day. I also went to night school to learn the language, and slowly but surely, I was becoming more fluent. Within three months I understood English when spoken to me, and within a year, I could speak English quite well. Little by little, I felt I was becoming more of an American!

One day, I decided to go to Manhattan to look around. I came back to the house and no one was home. I didn't have a key, so I was hanging around outside waiting for Regina and Morris. All of a sudden, a police car came by and asked me, "Who are you?" I took out my ID. The neighbors were complaining that someone was loitering. The policeman said, "You like beer? Go wait in the bar for them." I understood what he was telling me, but I couldn't speak any English to have a conversation with him, or to explain myself! So I did as he said, and went into the bar down the street until my sister was back home.

After two weeks I got a job in a factory on 5th Avenue, making belts for ladies' dresses, which were being sold to Woolworths, McCrories and Kreskie (which eventually became Kmart). It was mass production, putting holes in the belts. I remember, the holes had to be straight. It was very boring, repetitive work, and I made a total of $28.00/week for this grind. From the time I landed on American shores, I was always looking ahead, and figuring out what my next move would be, in order to get ahead, to make more money, to become financially independent and stable. I had ambition. After 2 months, I went to my boss, a Jewish man, and I asked him: "Do I have a future here?" He said "No." So I quit that day, and it wasn't long before I lined up another job making $40.00/week!

My brother in law, Morris Zola introduced me to ILGWU local 40 belt makers union representative Morris Fishbein. I went to him after I quit the 28.00/week job and said, "I need a job." He got me a job making leather belts, an upgrade from the plastic belts of my first employer. This time though, I was in a smaller factory. I was the only employee, just me and the boss. My boss, had old broken machines, and if one broke, he would tell me, "I need a screw for the machine. So, go to the hardware store and get a screw for me." I'd come back with the screw and he was so cheap he'd ask me, "What did you pay for it?" "A nickel," I'd tell him. "A nickel! I bought one yesterday for three cents", he'd complain!

He was also a Jewish guy, and he had a heart condition, which couldn't have been helped by how stressed he always was about his business. Well, one day he had a heart attack. His son took over, but his son didn't want to work. He would ask me, "Do you mind if we close at 2 PM?" I stayed in this job just for the summer, and then I left, and Morris found me another job in a big factory in Manhattan, also making belts. This place made belts for big accounts. I was doing the

same thing for them as my summer job, but I got a raise –
now, I was earning $45.00/week!

Meanwhile, I changed locations. My older brother Louis was
living in the Bronx, in the apartment Regina used to rent
before they bought their house. He was living with my
younger brother, Eddie. Louis was about to get married, but
he needed to find a place for Eddie to live. Right after the
war, apartments were very hard to find and were at a
premium. Louis and his new wife Loretta took over Regina's
old apartment. Frida arrived from Czechoslovakia with her
husband and their little boy. They got a three-bedroom
place in the Bronx in the same building where Louis and his
wife lived. They lived in two rooms, and my brother Eddie
and I lived in the third bedroom. The address was 500
Trinity Ave, in the Bronx.

One day, while at work, an idea occurred to me. I said
previously I was always thinking of getting ahead – how can
I make more money? I told the other guys working with me,
"You want to make more money? Watch me; play along
with me." I went to the boss, and I said, "look, you are

paying us this or that, and you don't know about the production. How about paying us by the piece?" He said okay and we settled on a price. I went back to the guys and told them, "guys, now you go faster - the more belts you make, the more money you make". We started to make $90 – $120/week, which was a fortune in those days, a whole lot better than the $28.00/week that I started with when I arrived in America! The boss was a real gentleman and I really liked working for him.

After a while, I decided I wanted to do another job in the belt business. Of course I wanted to make more money. I went to my friend Morris F. to help me again. Morris was able to get me another job in the belt industry, but this one was more skilled. I had to color the edges of the belt, being very careful with each one, and working at a table with paint, not sitting at a machine all day. I have to say, I didn't hate the work, and after a while I started making $10 – $12,000 a year. To put some perspective on this, I did some research on the Internet, and a yearly salary of $10,000 back in 1950s is equivalent to about $100,000 in today's salary. Not too shabby for a guy who never went to college and showed up off the boat not speaking a word of English!

My persistence and ambitions were paying off, literally. G-d bless America for giving me these opportunities!

I was making good money, and I had learned how to speak English. I was 31 years old, and it was time for me to get married. After living in America for about a year and a half, someone introduced me to my future wife, Rose. I had a friend who asked me, "Do you want to meet a girl?" He liked her but she didn't like him because he was too short! Some distant relatives had set them up. I called her house and we arranged a blind date. She lived in Brooklyn with her family. Her father, Mr. Abe Bunin, a Russian Jew in the construction business, liked me right away, and so did her mother, Tessie, who was born in Poland. Rose worked for the New York Times, in their accounting department. She was 24 and born in America. Some people might have wondered – how could I marry someone who was not a survivor, or a refugee? How would she ever understand what I had been through? Truthfully, I just wanted to live a normal life. She was a nice girl, very pretty, and she came from a stable home. Her mother and father were nice people. What more could I want?

Rose and I dated 7-8 months. We socialized a lot with friends, went to the movies, hung out in Brooklyn, and sometimes we'd just walk in the street on Eastern Parkway and Pitkin Ave. We socialized with some refugees and mostly Americans, because she had a lot of friends before we met.

I don't remember how I proposed to her, but I know I didn't get down on one knee! I know that she didn't refuse me!

We were married on January 6, 1951, in a wedding hall, Melrose Chateau, located in Brooklyn. Thankfully, the weather on our wedding day was beautiful. It was a pretty fancy wedding for the time, under a chuppah with her Rabbi, with all of her family and my surviving siblings and their families, and lots of friends. Of course it was kosher. My wedding day was almost two years to the day since I had arrived in America. It goes without saying that the loss of my parents was very painful to me on my wedding day. At that time, Holocaust survivors didn't talk about this pain. Until Eli Weisel wrote "Night" and other survivors wrote books, no one spoke about the Holocaust. Most survivors felt what is now referred to as "survivor's guilt." I felt the pain of this loss, but I discussed it with no one.

The next day, after the wedding, we went to the Catskill Mountains- "Borscht Belt" for our honeymoon (We had been there in the summertime when we were not yet married, but that time we were with her parents, and enjoyed it. I didn't have a car yet so we took a bus up there, and although we had been lucky with the weather for our wedding, we ran into a tremendous snowstorm. We were staying in one of the few hotels open in the winter, the Nevele Country Club, and about 90 percent of the guests were honeymooners! We met some people there whom we remained friends with for years.

The thing is, the bus doesn't bring you directly to the hotel. It had a regular route, not close to the hotel. In the middle of this snowstorm, we had to get from the bus stop to the hotel. They sent a car for us and we finally got there.

We honeymooned for a week, and then it was time to return to reality and our workweek.

My father-in-law owned a six family house in Brooklyn, and he gave us a 2 bedroom apartment to start off our married lives. We lived on Hendrix Street.

I was a happily married man, and stayed that way for sixty-two years, until I lost my dear Rose, a'h, on December 26, 2012. I miss her every day. I had a good feeling about her on the day I met her, and that feeling never changed, only grew stronger.

Chapter 7: Marriage, Kids, and Career

Two years after our wedding, almost to the day, our son Jeff was born, on January 11, 1953, while we were living in Brooklyn. I was in the hospital hallway and waiting room with my father-in-law while my wife was in labor. In those days, the fathers were not allowed in the delivery room. My wife liked to joke with me – "I was in labor, and you were out eating a corned beef sandwich!" She had a rough labor with my son – he had to be pulled out with forceps and ended up with some bruises on his forehead. His official name is Jeffrey Michael, named after my father. Then, they kept the woman and baby in the hospital for over a week! The bris, was on the eighth day and was performed in the hospital by a moyle. My siblings, whoever could make it, came to the hospital for the bris. Whenever I had any success in life, the feeling I had was, "I'm beating Hitler". I cheated Hitler until now and I'm cheating him again. No higher experience than having a child born could make me feel this more.

Rose had worked full time for the NY Times, until her seventh month but after she came home from the hospital with our son, she became a full-time housewife, as was the norm in the fifties. Rose was very frugal, and an excellent mother and household manager. We had a very traditional marriage, which suited me just fine. I worked, and she took immaculate care of the house, and of our children.

Our daughter Rochelle (everyone calls her Shelley) was born on the second day of Sukkos, October 13, 1954. I dropped Jeff, who was 21 months old, at my in-laws and then took my wife to the hospital. I went back to pick Jeff up to take him home and a phone call confirmed Shelley was already born! Her official name is Rochelle Shelley, named after my mother and my sister Shari who perished in the Holocaust. There were no issues with the delivery or birth. My wife stayed a week after the birth in the hospital, and my mother-in-law took care of Jeff, while my wife was in the hospital.

So now we were blessed with a son and a daughter! Shelley was an incredibly happy baby, easy to care for. She didn't cry a lot. My wife had her hands full though, taking care of two babies less than 2 years old. So, it's a good thing Shelley and Jeff were such good, happy babies! They even played together in the same playpen. We lived in a Brooklyn walk up with two flights of stairs. Just to bring the children outside was a big job for my wife with the baby carriage and all of the stuff she had to bring. And still, my wife was incredible. The children were immaculate all the time – they even wore white polished shoes every day! She always managed to keep our house just as immaculate as the children, and remarkably, whenever I came home from work, she had dinner waiting for me. All through our marriage, except when she became frail, my wife cooked for me. In the beginning she didn't know how to cook, but she learned!

When you go out walking with children, you meet other women and children in the same situation, and my wife had a lot of friends in the area with children the same age as ours. I will say though, as many friends as my wife had, she dedicated her life to our family, and the family's needs always came first before anything else.

During the mid-fifties, I kept on working in the company where I was polishing belts. I stayed with this company for ten years plus. I was really doing the top job there, and was the most responsible, so I stuck with it all those years. Now that I was a father, my ambitions were growing to create a business for myself instead of always working for someone else. I decided that it was time for me to venture out on my own, and the belt business is what I knew, so, that was a natural direction for me to go. While I was still working for my boss, I was negotiating in secret to take a 50% partnership in a belt manufacturing company. I must have been negotiating with the owner of this company for a year. Raymond (the owner) gifted the other half to his brother Harold.

When the negotiations were all done, I had another place to go. (I could never quit my job without having another one lined up). I went to see my boss on a Thursday and I told him, "I have to quit. It's time for me to leave." I told him I'd finish up the week, but he was flabbergasted. He asked me where I was going, but I was obligated to keep it a secret, so I told him, "I'm going into the belt business." My boss got so mad at me, he said, "Go now."

Should one who quits a job to better himself, feel guilty? I didn't feel guilty at this moment when I left the company. The only thing I felt bad about was that I was working with a guy there who helped me learn the business. During the years I was there, he stopped doing the actual work, and he depended on me. I felt bad about leaving him. He was devastated. We were very close friends, and my wife was close to his wife as well. After I left, he couldn't do the job, and he stopped talking to me for quite a few years. Eventually, he and his wife moved to Southern New Jersey. But, we resumed our friendship when one day I had to do business in Philadelphia, which was near his neighborhood. So, I invited him out to dinner. They even came to my childrens' weddings.

This was the sixties. I entered into a business that had been operating for at least 20 – 25 years. The factory, named Nord-Ray Belts Manufacturing, employed 35 people, and was located at 670 Broadway, North of Houston Street in a very busy part of the Village in Manhattan. We made and sold wholesale leather belts in a 10,000 square foot manufacturing facility. We bought leather from tanneries or wholesalers[6], and then sold the belts to the big chain stores and wholesalers. To buy our share of the business, Rose and I got no help from family, and didn't take out any loans. It all came from money we saved – remember I told you that Rose was very frugal! We paid $25,000 for that business – a real fortune in those days. How'd we do it? We lived a simple, prudent life. We didn't splurge. We went on vacations every year, for two weeks, to Miami in the winter.

---

[6] The previous owner bought a lot from a guy, Willy Rappaport, who had five factory floors of leather. He came to my business and asked for Ray, "the seller". I said, "Ray isn't here anymore, Harold and I took over the business." Then he told me that Ray owed him $80,000, which was a lot of money in the 60's! As the new owners we were responsible for that. So I said, "Look, Mr. Rappaport, if you will work with us, you will get paid." He said "ok, I'll work with you and if you need merchandise I'll give you more credit". Good to my word, I paid him off. He had a good customer in us

Otherwise, we saved every penny we could, because Rose understood and supported my ambitions and she managed our household with tremendous skill.

Truth is, I hated my partner, hated his guts, really, and I don't say that lightly. Why? because he was a crook. I am, and always have been, an honest man. My father was an honest man. I couldn't respect a man who was a thief, and he took a lot of money out of our business that wasn't rightfully his. He had all kinds of creative ways to grab money out of the company. For example, we paid the employees their salary by check every Tuesday. In those days, if you didn't have a bank account, the bank would charge you for cashing the paycheck. The union contract required that we pay for cashing these checks. We sent them to a cash checking outfit across the street, and they sent a bill every week for cashing all these checks. Maybe the bill was $25/week. At one point I began seeing bills from them for 2-3 hundred dollars every week. I asked the bookkeeper what this was about and she told me to just ask Harold. I found out, he was taking money orders for himself and lining his pockets!

He'd get a new company car, drive it for two months, and then we'd see a bill to replace the tires. He found so many ways to illegally sift money out of the company for his own use, it made me crazy. But still, we were making good money, and I didn't want to break up the business. I had to learn to live with it because I had no choice. I told myself, *"So, he steals $20,000 a year. Well, $10,000 of that is his anyway, and when you are in business for yourself, you get special perks, so it's like he's paying himself just $120.00/week more than he's supposed to be getting."* That was my rational but I didn't respect or trust the guy, and that's very difficult when you are partners. What I can say is I'm proud that I didn't become like him, and do the same shenanigans that he did. I was never tempted. That was not who I was. The only thing I allowed myself to do was to go on more elaborate vacations on the company's expense, but I would never steal or do anything illegal or underhanded.

Although I didn't enjoy working with my business partner, we were an excellent team, and we grew that business for 25 years becoming known for on-time delivery and high quality. In the sixties, we were doing a million and a half a year. After two years, we doubled the production with the same employees. My job was production manager, and I also did sales in the city. My business partner's job was running the office, and more or less, handling clients, which I did as well.

Eventually, after 25 years, I noticed the business profits were diminishing. We were tied up with unions which insisted that employees only work 35 hours/week, and 13% of every employee's yearly income had to be paid to the union to cover health and vacation benefits. One day, I called on an established customer who had really become like a friend. He said to me, "See these goods imported from Brazil, Taiwan, and China? They look like yours, but I can get them for a third less." I realized there was no way we could compete with manufacturing in China, which operated

---

[7] If not for Harold, I could be very wealthy today. The original owner of our building was in the millinery business when every woman wore a hat. His main customer was JC Penny and he lost the account. He came to us and said, "I'm selling the building for 400K." I told Harold we should buy it, but he had no foresight. He said, "We don't have the money". So I said, "We'll get a mortgage," I argued. "We're paying rent anyway". He wouldn't do it. That building is worth at least 20 million dollars now. But G-d gave me a much better plan, because I'm still alive and Harold died a long time ago!

without unions. That's when I decided it was time to get out of the business[7]. I could see what was coming. In 1985, I sold my half of the partnership to my partner. His wife and daughter were working there – he wouldn't sell out of the business, and they were very proud of it. (He ended up dying a year and a half after I sold it to him, and his wife ran the business for a while).

Along with the expense of purchasing the business, in 1958, Rose and I also purchased a new house for $20,000 in the Howard Beach development, which proved to be an ideal place to raise our family. We used savings Rose brought into our marriage and wedding gifts we saved, and were able to mortgage only $5000 with an FHA loan which we paid off in a few years.

Meanwhile, as I established myself as a successful entrepreneur, the family was growing up and thriving in Howard Beach. In the 1960's we helped build a shul there, fundraising over 1 million dollars (a lot of money now, but even more so in the 1960's). It was named the Rockwood Park Jewish Center, and was not only an Orthodox shul, but also a kosher catering establishment. I was very active there all the years we lived in Howard Beach. I was on the Board of Directors and I was very close to the Rabbi, Rafael Safra. I went to services regularly, and my wife joined me for special occasions. The shul was within walking distance of our home. It grew so large, that during the holidays there was no room, and we had to expand into the catering establishment.

Jeff had his bar mitzvah in this shul. He was very smart, and he layned the haftorah. He attended an after school Hebrew school – this was before day schools were popular. This was our first simcha as a family. Everyone in the family showed up for a big party. We had a big kiddish in the shul, and then a party at night in a catering hall.

The Howard Beach community was a place with a lot of friends for both of our children. When we first moved in, it wasn't fully developed. There were lots of sandy land fill areas where Jeff and other kids played baseball. On one of those fields Jeff wound up with a broken nose when someone threw a ball smack into his nose. I was home at the time and took him to a doctor who was a friend in the community. He directed me to take Jeff to the Ear Nose and Throat hospital in Manhattan. He had to have surgery to fix his broken nose. This was when he was pre-bar mitzvah, and till this day his nose gives him some trouble.

Jeff graduated from John Adams High School and from there went to college at NYU. He had excellent grades and it was a very competitive college to get into. NYU Washington Square was very near my business. After school, he came up, and he did some of his homework and we went home together. He lived at home, which was about an hour's drive away. I was very grateful that he drove, because after a whole day's work, I was tired.

One day after NYU, he's hanging around at our work, and I saw a card that said he made the dean's list. I asked him, "Why didn't you tell me?" He said, " it's nothing". This is how he is. He never wants to talk about himself or show off. I admire his integrity. I'm so proud of him. He's a prominent man in his shul and the community. He graduated from Downstate Medical School in Brooklyn where he received his medical degree. He did his residency at Monmouth Medical Center, specializing as an internist. He met another doctor there, Rich Miller, and after they finished their residency, they came down to Florida and opened a practice together, and they are still business partners today. They get along famously. His practice is located in Holiday, Florida, and they are primary care physicians. He's board certified in internal medicine and geriatrics and has been recognized for excellence in his field by his society. They have a very busy office and they own their building. Even today, till this day, his integrity is rare and impeccable.

I have a son, and a daughter, and a daughter-in-law, and to me, they are all the same. My daughter in law, Susan, considers me like a father, and I consider her my daughter. They met in New Jersey when he was in residency, and she was a cardiac nurse. She was not Jewish, and today she is more Jewish than most Jewish people. She is 100 percent kosher. She's a Jew like she was born Jewish. They married on July 24, 1983. The wedding was in a Jewish Center in Queens. Susan went through conversion before the wedding through an Orthodox Rabbi that I spoke with. Susan and Jeff talked with him and a couple days later he called me at work and said, "Mazel Tov, I'll do it for you. She is sincere." I wanted to make sure she didn't just want to marry a Jewish doctor! She wanted to be Jewish. He converted her. It's very important for my family.

Right after they married, they moved down to Florida, on July 24, 1983. We were still living up north then. They had foresight, and wanted to settle some place nice to raise a family and to start a practice. After a couple of years, they bought land and built their own office.

Jeff and Susan are very active in shul now. Young Israel Chabad of Pinellas County, located in Palm Harbor is where we daven, and we've been involved ever since Chabad came to town. Before that we belonged to a Conservative shul, Beth Shalom. I was on the Board of Directors there too. I still go there sometimes during the week, but we switched over to Chabad, which was Susan's doing, because she enjoyed the orthodox service more. Susan loves Israel, loves Shabbos, and is a true Jew!

My wife and I had Friday night Shabbos dinner by Jeff and Susan practically every single week, and enjoyed her homemade challah and all that she prepared. (Sometimes we would go to a close friend, changing off sometimes).

Aaron, my grandson, was born on December 1, 1984, in Florida. This was my first grandchild and it was a very big deal. We were living in New York at the time, and we came down to Florida for the bris, which took place in a friend's house.

I was very proud. Aaron's bris repaired something in my heart.

We saw a lot of my grandson while we were up north because we got together for the holidays, either up north or in Florida. When we moved to Florida part-time as snowbirds, we got to see him a lot more. In 2006, we moved full time to Florida.

I have the most special relationship with my grandson Aaron. First of all, he is something special. After they made him, they threw away the mold. Aaron is an Ophthalmologist. When he applied to the Ophthalmology program, (USF) there were only four slots, and two hundred applicants; he made one of them. He's a real high achiever. He's 31 years old and already he has his own office. There is no show off about him and yet he is so well respected.

He has always been respectful of us. If there was anything going on in the family he always asks, "will Grandpa be there?" Aaron is married to a wonderful girl, Jennifer, whom he met at the Chabad in Gainesville, where he went to medical school. She is just like him, and I am very close to her as well. She is a dentist in a group practice. She is a Ger (convert), and much like her mother in law, she has embraced Judaism fully. Aaron and Jennifer are a great match, matched up in heaven. They just got married in January, 2015.

I see my grandson and Jennifer most Friday nights for Shabbos dinner, and I often talk to my grandson during the week.

I also have two granddaughters by Jeff and Susan. Alexis, was adopted as an infant, and Laura, who was also adopted as an infant.

Laura is also very special to me. Laura lives in Gainesville, and is 21 years old. She went on a Jewish heritage tour of Poland and currently is in Israel learning Hebrew and Israeli culture. She is a talented photographer. When she is home, I see her on Friday nights for Shabbos. Laura and I have a very wonderful relationship. I know she likes me and I love her very much. As a matter of fact, she has called me numerous times from Israel! I miss her very much. Hopefully she will meet someone and get married.

Laura has a very big heart and loved her grandma very dearly. On one of her last nights, Laura sat by her bed and held her hand. She is wonderful.

Alexis has brought all of us a beautiful child, whose name is Rylee. She has spent many Shabbats with us, and she is just a joy for all of the family.

She is named for Rose, Shana Razel.

I have been blessed with such special children. I've shared with you how much respect and appreciation I have for Jeff and his family. I feel so fortunate as well to be close to my daughter Shelley. She went to Queens College in NY as an undergraduate and went on to receive a Master's Degree in Special Education from NYU. She teaches children with learning impairments and has many success stories. She finds her work to be very gratifying. She married Arthur Trachtenberg in New York as a young adult. We celebrated a nice wedding under the chuppah in the same place where Jeff and Susan were married a year later. Arthur worked as a CPA. Sadly, they got divorced after 28 years, but they still talk to each other almost every week, and he still calls me once in a while and still refers to me as "Dad."

Shelley and Art adopted one son, whose name is Steven. It was rewarding for Rose and I to have been able to spend our summers in an apartment in Rego Park, New York. There we were able to spend a lot of quality time with

Shelley and her family who lived in a home not far away, in Valley Stream. We got to be with Steven for all of his milestones. We loved our times spent together. He went to a Jewish Day School in Lawrence, NY and learned a lot. He was an excellent davener. Steven has been a volunteer firefighter since he was in high school. He works for 2 different firehouses as a paid employee. I am proud of him as well as all of my grandchildren. He has recently been to Israel on Birthright and is anxious to go back. He is passionate about his volunteer firehouse position and now is a captain. He lives with his father. My daughter sees Steven often, either visiting him in New York or when he visits us in Florida.

I am very close to my daughter Shelley. We speak maybe 5-6 times a day. Sometimes, she'll just pop over during the week and we'll put a steak on the barbecue and enjoy dinner together. First thing when she gets up in the morning, she calls me. She moved down to Florida after she divorced, and now lives only a 15-minute drive from me. She's an elementary school teacher and has a tutoring practice. Shelley is very dedicated to me, and she's a very honest and wonderful person. Her integrity and kindness are rich. Everyone who knows her loves her, and I understand why!

How fortunate am I, to live such a long life, with a dedicated wife, and to be close to my children, and my grandchildren. I have lived to see a great granddaughter, enjoying their company, and the nachas they give me. This is The Best Revenge on Hitler there ever will be!

Chapter 8: Greeting Cards and Retirement

When I sold the belt business, I was too young to retire. I was used to working all day long, and I was bored. I was in good health and about 67 years of age. Maybe for some people that's retirement age – but I was still vigorous and healthy. I also wanted to find another opportunity to earn money. I had a neighbor who knew that I was looking for something new. He suggested we go into the greeting cards and gift business. Back then, greeting cards were a big thing – you couldn't find them in a supermarket or drugstore like you can today.

I knew nothing about this business. My neighbor, Mr. Oberfield, went to the same synagogue as I did. He had just sold a business and he was looking for a new one, but he was looking for a partner. He said to me, "Let's go into the greeting cards and gifts business together." He would be the expert, because he had been in that kind of business before, and I would put in some cash and help him run it.

We walked all over Manhattan looking for the right location; I'm surprised I had any soles left on my shoes! Finally, we settled on a place, Midtown in the garment district on, 37th street near 7th Ave. Next door was a famous kosher restaurant.

We spent $150,000 to buy the lease and fix up the store. We started with an empty store that once sold cigars, but we didn't want to sell cigars, (although we did sell cigarettes) so it took quite a bit of renovating to make it a presentable greeting cards store. "Cards and Gifts Incorporated" was our name. We sold greeting cards, cigarettes, and there was a lotto machine (lottery). I ran the store for two years.

Let me tell you – my first business partner in the leather belt business was a *ganif* (crook). My second business partner was an honest man, but when it came to business, he was stupid! My partner didn't understand how to make money in retail. He'd go to the wholesalers and buy one of a kind. I couldn't believe it. I tried to explain to him – "you can't make any money if you only buy one of everything! Why don't you buy a dozen at a time?" But I couldn't get him to change his ways. We sold cigarettes, and we were constantly running out of the cigarettes that our customers wanted, because the salesman only came once a week. What kind of a way is that to run a business?

After two years of trying to make it work, and making no headway with my business partner, I got disgusted, and I told him I wanted to sell it. Manhattan rent was very high and we weren't making enough money for all this work and aggravation. He wanted out of it too. He contacted a business broker, but it was taking too long. My partner told me, "that's it, next week, we're closing up." But I told him not to close up so fast. I put an advertisement in the NY Times to sell the store. Just a few days later, an interested Chinese couple came into the store, I negotiated with them and we sold it to them on the spot. They gave us a down payment, and then made monthly payments to us. Unfortunately, they discovered a few years later that it wasn't so easy to make money in this business, and they decided to close if when they still owed my partner and me a few thousand dollars.

Unfortunately, the greeting card venture was not successful but fortunately, during that time, I was able to support the family with stock investments, and no one was starving. It was a lesson learned. From that point on, no more business partnerships in my life!

By the time I got out of the greeting card business, our children were grown and independent, out of the house, and there was no longer any reason for us to remain in New York. The house was long paid off and worth quite a bit of money. We sold the house and we purchased a condominium in Clearwater Florida, and an apartment in Forest Hills to live in during the summertime. My son Jeff and his wife were living in Florida at that time, and we wanted to live close to them.

When we moved to Florida, I was 70, and I wasn't quite ready to retire. I looked around for stores to buy. It was hard for me to get the entrepreneurial bug out of my system. I'm glad I didn't buy anything. Eventually I just accepted being retired, and I spent a lot of my time reading, and studying what I needed to know to manage our investments.

Rose and I thoroughly enjoyed our life in Florida. Eventually, in 2006, we sold our apartment in New York and lived full time in Florida. We really had a great life together there, enjoying very close relationships with our grown children and grandchildren. Shelley and her family in the winter visited often. We enjoyed extensive travel together, Yellowstone, California, Washington and Oregon and so many more. In 2000 Rose and I took our fourth trip to Israel with Jeff, Sue and Aaron.

We lived in Forest Hills, New York, for about 6 months. During that time we visited family and took a trip with Shelley, Art, and Steven. This apartment was about 30 minutes from Shelley's home. How fortunate Rose and I were to have children who "fought" over us to stay longer!

Then, Rose got was diagnosed with CLL, a form of Leukemia. She became frail and had numerous problems. She had a stomach operation that didn't go well, and then developed trouble walking, so I started taking over the house chores, and a woman came in to the apartment to help us. I was taking care of her, and the house, the best I could. Then one day, in March, 2012, Rose collapsed near the bathroom.

Shelly called for an ambulance and she was rushed to the hospital where she was diagnosed with pneumonia. She was hospitalized for a week, and from then on, she never came home again. First she went to rehabilitation for one month, and then she needed to live in an assisted living facility. We needed to find a kosher place for Rose, and the closest one was about a 40-minute drive away, run by the Jewish Federation. Rose needed help 24-hours a day, so we lived separately for about 10 months. I visited her every day unless I had a cold. Rose was beloved in that place. She was so likeable, and everyone loved her there. She was always kissing and hugging everyone. She had a touch of Alzheimers towards the end of her life but she always knew who her family was.

One day, I came to see her, as I did every afternoon, and I felt that something was not right. She wasn't smiling like she usually did. Then she stopped eating. My son guided me to hospitalize her. She was in the hospital 3-4 days, before they transferred her to hospice. She passed away in hospice at 5 AM. We were all with her when she passed on December 26, 2012. (Her yahrtzeit is the 13th of Tevet).

I visit my wife's grave every Friday afternoon. My whole life was focused on her, and losing her has been a major adjustment. I still live in the same condominium we shared, and I still see her walking around the place here. I always think, *how would Rose do this?* I still have some of her clothes in the condo that I don't part with.

Losing Rose has been far worse than anything I ever suffered, even in the Holocaust. We were married for more than sixty-two years – the best decision I ever made!

Thank God for my two dedicated children, my daughter in law, and my grandchildren. My ongoing involvement with

Chabad, the Shabbos rituals, and my close daily connections with my family has made widowhood easier to bear, and made my long years still very joyful.

I thank G-d every day that I walk around in good health, which allows me to do so many of the activities I do. I still drive a car, go to the gym, shop, visit with people – I have my independence and a very full life. I have been very blessed indeed.

Let me tell you something - I am very close to my brother, Eddie, my youngest brother. His life has been very tragic. In the Holocaust, he was recruited into the working battalion like me. But, instead he wound up in Mauthausen concentration camp in Austria for 4-5 months. I fortunately, managed to stay clear of the concentration camps. Eddie was very sick from typhus when he got out. I followed him to America after we met up with each other in Frankfurt. He married a woman from Sighet, Pearl Turner, and they had two children, Robin and Jeff. Pearl was a very nice lady. Tragically, she got breast cancer when their kids were young and she passed away in her late forties when Eddie was still a young man. I was fortunate enough to spend sixty two years with my Rose! Eddie was left to bring up two children. He remarried a woman younger than him, Ruth. They had some good years together. However, she developed Alzheimer's and went to live with her daughter in Boca Raton. So he was unlucky the second time around as well.

Jeff, Eddie's son became a cardiologist where he was a senior partner, and was a very prominent doctor. One Saturday night, Jeff was at a sixtieth birthday party in Manhattan for one of the first cousins and he said he didn't feel well and had trouble breathing. He left the party early himself not feeling well. He died before the ambulance came. To this day, I don't know the exact cause. Shelley was there, and she called my son Jeff after it happened to give him the terrible news. Jeff called me on the next morning and asked me to come over to discuss "something". He was afraid to tell me, but he did, and I got right on a plane and went to the funeral, and I stayed all the way through the shiva. Eddie's son Jeff was one of the apples of my brother's eye.

If Jeff's passing wasn't devastating enough, a couple of years later, Eddie's daughter Robin was diagnosed with ovarian cancer, and she passed away at a young age. Needless to say, it was catastrophic. Unimaginable losses, just heartbreaking. My brother was left all alone, a tragic ending to a very difficult life. But, there is only one thing that saves him now – his grandchildren from Jeff, and Jeff's wife, Sue, who takes care of him like her own father. He is in a Kosher assisted living facility near her and I bless her, every day, how well she takes care of him. She is truly his guardian angel! He would not be able to exist without her care.

Why did I merit to live such a long healthy life, and to be able to enjoy being married to Rose for 62 years, and to still relish being close to Jeff, Shelley, their spouses, and my grandchildren? I have no answer to this question.

My dear sister Frida and her husband Ari married on December 7 ,1941 both survived Auschwitz . They immigrated from Czechoslovakia in the early 1950s. She too developed colon cancer at a young age and died in her mid-

50s a day before Rosh Hashanah. Her last words were about her desire to go home to prepare for the holidays. I will never forget the last time I saw her in the hospital.

I would be remiss if I didn't write something about my sister Regina and her husband Morris. Regina and my brother in law Morris were wonderful people. When the situation in Europe was getting bad, they sent my father money when his business was ordered to be shut down. Morris himself didn't have a lot of money. They did more for the family than anyone can imagine. They actually helped keep us from starvation. Regina, while visiting Frida in Czechoslovakia, gave me money so that I could make my way to Germany and the American Zone in 1947.

Throughout the years, Regina and Morris' home was open to us for all holidays and get-togethers. Regina and Morris were like surrogate parents to me. Even when I got engaged to Rose, they invited my future in laws to their home for dinner – just like parents.

I have tremendous gratitude for all that I have been blessed with, none of which I ever take for granted. This life I have been living, is truly the best revenge!

Postscript

It is my fervent hope after reading this book that it has made an impact on you. I am privileged to have edited this manuscript and in so doing had the opportunity to help flesh out the details of stories I have heard before but never with such clarity and depth. The story of survival and transcendence by dad from a time of despair armed only with hope, with determination, and faith is immortal and the story of human survival. Certainly Providence had much to do with survival but without a positive attitude the best of luck would not have been adequate.

Dad's family members who made it through were very special, living life with gusto not dwelling on the Holocaust. Each one struggled with their own demons but never to the detriment of their families. This is a story of personal fortitude, an amazing story that makes our trials and tribulations today trivial by comparison.

This book is our family heirloom to future generations. A gift to those who care to connect and explore. It is a looking glass into the past, and a warning to those who do not learn the essential lessons of history. Finally, here is a tribute to victory, triumph over evil, rebirth, repair and renewal that brings joy to all our hearts.

Many thanks to all those who have helped put together this living legacy.

- Jeff

Reflecting back, I am certain that my dad's temperament, personality, strength, and resolve aided in his survival, and his ability to continue living a full life.

Growing up, (and even now) I knew that I could always depend on Dad for sound advice. He seemed to always have the attitude that "it's not so bad" or "let's see what can be done another way". Nothing seemed insurmountable to him. I'm sure his experiences in the war, helped to shape his attitudes about life.

Dad never let these horrific events hold him back from helping my mom raise my brother Jeff and I, with clear vision, sound advice, and a great sense of humor.

Even today, he is the "rock" of the family, and I know that my mom felt the same way.

My dad put all of his heart and soul into his family (including his siblings). He also directed his feelings into giving to charities and to his relentless support of Israel. His motto, even until this day, has been "never give up hope…".

- Shelley

61643886R00117

Made in the USA
Lexington, KY
28 March 2017